LITERARY STRUCTURES

Edited by John Gardner

The Construction
of Christian Poetry
in Old English

by

John Gardner

SOUTHERN ILLINOIS UNIVERSITY PRESS
Carbondale and Edwardsville

Feffer & Simons, Inc.
London and Amsterdam

Library of Congress Cataloging in Publication Data
Gardner, John Champlin, 1933–
   The construction of Christian poetry in Old English.

   (Literary structures)
   Includes bibliographical references and index.
   1. Anglo-Saxon poetry—History and criticism.
2. Christian poetry, Anglo-Saxon—History and criticism.
I. Title.
PR201.G37   829'.1   74-28475
ISBN 0-8093-0705-7

To my teacher, John C. McGalliard

Contents

Preface

In the past decade, a number of first-rate books and articles have appeared which deal with fine details of the construction of poetry in Old English, including—to mention only a few of the best and most recent—Neil D. Issacs' *Structural Principles in Old English Poetry* (Knoxville, Tennessee, 1968), B. F. Huppé's *The Web of Words: Structural Analyses of the Old English Poems, Vainglory, The Wonder of Creation, The Dream of the Rood, and Judith* (Albany, N.Y., 1970), and Alvin A. Lee's *The Guest-Hall of Eden: Four Essays on the Design of Old English Poetry* (New Haven, 1972). All these books and others, as well as numerous articles I'll have occasion to cite later, have made an accepted commonplace of what might have seemed incredible to most medievalists twenty years ago: that the bulk of Anglo-Saxon poetry, from *Beowulf* to the briefest of Cynewulfian poems, is poetry of the highest order of intelligence and aesthetic sophistication. No one was surprised twenty years ago when new, ever more complex interpretations of *Beowulf* came out (though some scholars, like Professor Kenneth Sisam, were dismayed); today no one is especially surprised when Huppé proves, as he does in *The Web of Words,* that the seemingly clumsy *Vainglory* is a brilliantly controlled work of art. Indeed, when we encounter a seemingly bad poem in Old English these days we shake our heads in confusion and struggle to discern its hidden merit.

There are of course bad poems in Old English; nevertheless, it is clear that most of the surviving Anglo-Saxon poetry is extraordinarily good, once we understand it. And so what seems useful now is new

avenues to understanding. My purpose in this book is to explore one
such avenue, what I call, for lack of a better term, Anglo-Saxon allegorical "styles"—the basic means by which early English Christian
poets tried to achieve what every serious poet seeks: resonance, depth
of vision, power. In some of what I say here my findings overlap with
the findings of others. For instance, my reading of Caedmonian poetry
and *Beowulf* leads me to conclusions identical to those of Alvin Lee
and others (notably E. G. Stanley and R. F. Leslie), though I arrive
where they arrive by a completely different route. In some cases my
corroboration of other people's discoveries has proved positively
startling, at least to me. When I began applying my method to *Beowulf*
I was in total disagreement with Professor Lewis Nicholson; when I
finished I was amazed that so seemingly haphazard an approach as his
could have reached my own brilliant conclusions. There is no justice.

Though I stumble, here and there, into an original reading, this
book's great virtue is not, I think, originality of interpretation but (to
some extent at least) originality of approach. I study Anglo-Saxon
allegorical styles in a systematic way, avoiding all presuppositions, however well-grounded the usual presuppositions may be historically,
working from the poem to the theory and not the reverse. Or, more
precisely, I make only those assumptions I make when I am writing
a novel or a long poem—assumptions about how a writer can com-
municate meaning without directly stating it. I watch sharply for
signals in the poem at hand, then try to figure out what the signals
are signalling. This leads me to theories of allegorical method, which
I then check in two ways: 1) does the same method also appear elsewhere in Old English poetry? and 2) is this apparent allegorical method
possible or probable in the poet's time and place? Which is to say,
of course, that I work here as all careful critics work, trying to respond
intelligently to the poem, catching its intellectual and emotional sub-
tleties, and that what I concentrate on more than anything else is the
signal which pushes the poem in the direction of allegory. My concern,
finally, is with the different kinds or *styles* of allegory, how each one
works and how several work when brought together in a single poem.
Thus this book has, really, two completely distinct but intrinsicate
purposes: the understanding of allegory's kinds, and the understanding
of particular poems in Old English. If I come up with, at times, more
or less standard interpretations of the poems, my isolation of the
several allegorical styles available to the Anglo-Saxon scop is new and,
I hope, interesting—as useful to the modern novelist or poet (not that
many will read this) as to the student of Old English verse.

To avoid needless confusion (or by way of apology for inviting confusion) let me explain—somewhat ponderously, alas—that as I use the word *style*, it means any regular departure from some norm of language. Strictly speaking, needless to say, "normal language" does not exist; but it seems self-evident that poetry at any time is in certain ways stylistically different from ordinary speech, and that, within any given time and place, poets of a particular school may be found to be more like one another stylistically than they are like poets of some other school of approximately the same time and place. This book, as I've said, explores a few of the ways in which all Anglo-Saxon Christian poems are similar and studies certain regular variations within the norm of Anglo-Saxon poetic style, the variations which make poetic movements.

Since poetic expression may differ from everyday prose expression not only in its choice of ornaments but also in its choice of methods of organization—its disposition and amplification of materials—I use the word *style* in a broad sense embracing not only verbal pattern but also structural design. I do not mean that the words *style* and *structure* are synonymous; I mean that just as one can speak of a poet's style in handling sentences, one can speak of characteristic styles of organization. For instance, the Mesopotamian preference for elaborating descriptions and set speeches but hurrying over major actions is a matter of style. So too John Donne's habit of developing an old analogy to its last logical extension is a part of Donne's poetic style.

Theoretically, stylistic analysis can suggest solutions to a variety of problems—questions of authorship and date, questions of influence and poetic evolution, problems in interpretation. My only concern here is with stylistic keys to interpretation. Stylistic keys, tested by interpretation, can provide a means of approaching any poem in Anglo-Saxon (I examine only a few) and should therefore be of broader value than specific answers to, say, authorship questions—questions which cannot be answered with finality until we know far more than we do at present about the whole corpus of poetry in Old English.

My method is close analysis of the style of individual poems, analysis which tries to discover, intuitively and empirically, the relationship of the given poem's parts and, later, the relationship of the given poem to the poetic tradition. When it is useful, I compare the poet's treatment of his material with the treatment in his source or in close analogues, and in this way I determine whether or not the poet makes consistent changes, giving clues to his object in writing his own version. I try to show that the poet's changes are explainable in terms of the rhetorical theory available to him, and that the poet's apparent purpose is consistent with the apparent purposes of other writers of his time. In general my analysis of style in any poem is concerned partly with vocabulary—a common concern of earlier studies—and partly with concepts and standard modes of expression. In religious poetry this often involves study of traditional religious "types" and forms of verbal repetition which indicate the poet's continuing interest in a few basic ideas throughout the poem. In my analysis of the language of a poem, I consider the connotations of particular words and the precise implications of figurative expressions. When I find that language seems to suggest a metaphorical relationship, for instance one between Christian experience and the pre-Christian Teutonic experience celebrated in the earlier "heroic" verse, I try to determine whether the metaphor is intended to be noticed or is simply frozen language. Here the tests are partly consistency and coherence within the poem, partly the practice of related poets. When a particular metaphor—such as the metaphor of earthly life as exile—appears in various poems and frequently comes couched in similar language or closely related half-lines, it becomes necessary to examine the possibility that the metaphor is a poetic convention of the poet's time and should be treated as carrying the same significance when it appears in more subtle poetic contexts.

A study as broad as this one must inevitably raise as many questions as it answers. What I offer is a theory and some notes toward a test of the theory. I deal not with all Christian poetry in Old English but only with those poems, from each major school, that I happen to like best; and for the readings I present I offer not full justification but only (as all sober judgment will agree) proof that the reading is plausible and helpful. To present more detailed analysis and more elaborate defense of my point of view, I would have to sacrifice my map of the forest for a wandering among trees.

I thank the editors of the following journals for permission to reprint here, in altered form, essays originally published in their pages: "Cynewulf's *Elene:* Sources and Structures," *Neophilologous* 54 (1970), 65–76; and "Fulgentius's *Expositio Vergiliana Continentia* and the Plan of *Beowulf:* Another Approach to the Poem's Style and Structure," *Papers on Language and Literature* 6 (1970), 227–62.

John Gardner

Carbondale, Illinois
1974

1

Premises

The Scop and the Rhetoricians

Undoubtedly Anglo-Saxon scops worked with formal poetic principles in mind; but if so, no trace of their theory has survived except as it is embodied in specific poems. Neither have we any sure knowledge of what the scop's training may have been. Bede's story of Caedmon, like other stories of the harp passed from hand to hand, suggests that some, at least, may have learned their art incidentally; but the artistry of Caedmon's *Hymn* makes us suspicious, to say the least, of Bede's informant. Other scops may have learned their skill through some form of apprenticeship. But we may be confident that the scop's knowledge was not always limited to traditional technique. Men like Aldhelm—who was skillful in composing vernacular songs both sacred and profane, according to Bede—must have had knowledge of classical and Christian rhetorical theory.[1]

As recent scholarship has made clear, book-learning is everywhere evident in Old English poetry, and not just in Caedmonic verse and the more self-consciously intellectual riddles. The *Beowulf*-poet was acquainted not only with Northern legends but also, almost certainly, with something like the *Liber Monstruarum*, with Virgil or Virgilian commentary, and with various patristic works. Cynewulf's breadth of knowledge is, of course, a commonplace of scholarship. None of this should surprise us. If an Anglo-Saxon with poetic talent entered the trivium, his studies taught him both how to interpret poetry and how to write it. His first course of study, *grammatica*, went beyond the thorough study of grammar. Marius Victorinus, one of the grammarians whose work was known in England, defines grammatica as "scientia interpretandi poetas atque historicos et recte scribendi loquendique ratio."[2] Servius, also available in England, has a similar definition, and Priscian apparently agrees, nearly all his grammatical illustrations coming from poetry.[3] The student learned more difficult matters of composition later, in his pursuit of *dialectica* and *rhetorica*.

Admittedly, early Church writers at times looked askance at rhetoric. Augustine, master rhetorician and rhetoric teacher, praised the rhetoric in St. Paul, called for logic and persuasive eloquence in preaching, but warned against excessive concern with rhetorical ornamentation, which might easily slide into sophistry and a greater concern with the letter than with the sense.[4] But despite its reservations, religion made rhetoric prosper, primarily for two reasons: first, rhetoric gave insight into the Bible and other works as well, and, second, rhetoric gave Christians a means of competing (both on the town bridge and in the pulpit, as Aldhelm found) with the pagans.

By the seventh century, non-Christians had long used the allegorical method to defend and justify pagan fables which might on a "superficial" level seem morally trivial or perverse; and Christians had by this time long made use of allegory both as a means of explaining difficult scripture and as a means of moralizing mythology or other old pagan materials for didactic purposes.[5] The allegorical reading of prophetic pagans like Virgil could be, according to Abelard, an act of religious devotion.[6] Such views were commonplace well before Abelard's time. There were those in Europe and in England as well—Gregory of Tours, Alcuin, and Herbert, Bishop of Norwich, for instance—who objected to Virgil and his kind as guides for Christians, but the effect of such attacks, even when they were in earnest (as Alcuin's jibe at his students was not) was negligible. The tradition behind the allegorical reading of pagan poets was too old and too firmly established to be overthrown.

From the medieval point of view, the outstanding example of the allegorical approach to pagan literature was the work of Fabius Fulgentius, whose work (*Mitologiarum* and *Expositio Vergiliana Continentia,* published in the late fifth or early sixth century) was represented in Ælbert's library as catalogued in Alcuin's verses on the Saints of York. There had been, before Fulgentius' commentary on Virgil, an earlier allegorical reading of the *Aeneid,* that of Aelius Donatus, and probably even Donatus' work was no new venture but an elaboration of an accepted approach.[7] One of Donatus' ideas, preserved by Servius, curiously foreshadows Fulgentius' commentary on the

Aeneid and perhaps casts doubt, not that it matters, on Fulgentius' originality. Virgil composed the *Bucolics,* then the *Georgics,* and finally the *Aeneid,* Donatus says, in imitation of the life of man, which moves through analogous conditions.[8] If Donatus saw the same three states worked out in the *Aeneid,* then Fulgentius' reading of the poem was already standard, at least in general outline, when it appeared. But the question is, as I say, of no great importance. The number of surviving manuscripts of Fulgentius' work, together with the praise given it throughout the Middle Ages, is proof that Fulgentius' scheme came to be, if it was not already in Fulgentius' day, the stock medieval reading of Virgil's epic. Because of the Christian and moralistic interpretation given to his work—an interpretation supported in the medieval mind by Virgil's apparent prophesy of Christ's birth in the fourth Eclogue—Virgil became among medieval Christians the most highly respected, most frequently quoted, and most intensely studied of all classical poets. (He is cited far more often in the rhetoric books of the Middle Ages than Homer, Ovid, or any other ancient, though many others—especially Ovid—came to be allegorized.) This allegorical reading of the pagans, which meant, in effect, their exoneration, was to open the way to frank imitation of their work.

Fulgentius was by no means the only such critic known in England. Alcuin's catalogue lists Cassiodorus, whose *Institutiones Divinarum et Humanarum Litterarum*—an encyclopedia of sacred and profane literature (together with other matter)—must certainly have been known in many parts of England. Victorinus, Servius, Priscian, and Donatus the grammarian were also known. Neither in his catalogue nor anywhere else does Alcuin mention Martianus Capella, textbook of the Irish schools, master allegorist and imitator of Virgil; but Englishmen familiar with Irish monastic learning either in Ireland or in England, where it was well represented, must certainly have encountered his work. In the books of any of these grammarians and rhetoricians, Englishmen could learn to understand and appreciate classical and Christian poetry, both its larger meanings (as then understood) and its subtler devices. And a good supply of such poetry was available in England, besides Christian poets, Virgil, Statius, Lucan, and probably—among the "alios perplures . . . magistros" whom Alcuin did not list—Ovid, Horace, and Terence, all quoted by the English. And new books were continually arriving as a result of English visits to Rome and France—the travels of Benedict Biscop, for example, who went six times to Rome, bringing back, among other treasures, "magna copia . . . voluminum sacrorum."

Knowledge of classical and early Christian poetry, knowledge of poetry's rhetorical and grammatical principles, and love of classical masters like Virgil soon led to imitation both in Latin and in the vernacular. A brief review of this tradition, familiar though the material may be, will prove useful. In the beginning, Christian poetry did not ordinarily seek to adapt pagan fables to Christian use but, borrowing classical meters and colors, sought to supplant or destroy things pagan. Prudentius's hexameters in the first book of *Contra Symmachum* (late fourth century) attack the pagan gods as nonsensical lies. His greatest work, to medieval taste, the *Psychomachia*, shows the struggle between Christendom against paganism under the transparent allegory of a struggle between Christian virtues and pagan vices—personified abstractions. Elsewhere he uses the classical poetic devices for thoroughly Christian subject matter, writing eulogies to martyrs, hymns, and so forth.

In the writing of the fourth-century Spanish priest Juvencus and those who follow him, Christian poetry takes another tack. Juvencus' *Historia Evangelica* (*Libri Evangeliorum IV*), written around 330, presents the gospel story in four books of hexameters recalling Virgil. His prologue, which speaks on the lies of Homer and Virgil, shows the motivation of Prudentius and his like, but Juvencus' use of biblical narrative points a new direction. The same tack was taken by Claudius Marius Victor, near the middle of the fifth century, in *Alethia,* three books of commentary on Genesis, written in hexameters —a verse translation interrupted by didactic digressions. More interesting books of the same type followed. One was the *Paschale Carmen* of Sedulius, a poem in five books put together with a solid knowledge of classical *inventio*—selection of the right materials for the elaboration of a theme. Sedulius tells key Old Testament stories of miraculous deliverance, turns to the birth and childhood of Christ, then deals with the saving "miracula Christi," the paschal sacrifice, and the redemption. In the closing years of the fifth century came a still freer biblical poem, Dracontius' *De Deo*. Dracontius tells of his own grim situation as a prisoner to the Vandal King Gunthamund and plays this personal narrative against biblical stories of God's mercy and stories from pagan antiquity. An even more impressive poem came soon afterward (early sixth century) from Avitus of Gaul—*De Spiritalis Historiae Gestis*. The first three sections of Avitus' work, dealing imaginatively with the fall of man, may have influenced the English Caedmonic poet who treated this subject and may also have influenced Milton. Juvencus and Sedulius are on Alcuin's list, and probably others of this group were known at York.

As the examples of Prudentius and Dracontius show, the transfer of classical techniques to Christian subject matter was not limited to biblical translation. Hymns, saints' lives, and other types of poetry were common, and all can without much difficulty be viewed as Christian counterparts to—or substitutions for—classical poetic types. The Christian poet's motivation was no doubt as conscious, in most cases, as it was for Hroswitha of Gandersheim (tenth century) who, by her own account, wrote plays on the martyrdom of saints because the pleasant language of Terence's immoral comedies seduced the innocent and demanded a wholesome substitute in similar dramatic form.[9]

But not all Christian poetry sought to root out pagan material and replace it with things Christian. Pagan heroes and pagan stories might themselves be turned to Christian use. Some of the stories which at an early date accumulated around the lives of saints or of Christ himself are clearly transferred from pagan legend. A striking example is the story of the Gautama Buddha, Bosiphata, who came into the Western languages as Josaphat or Johosiphat, and whose guide, Balaam, turned into a Christian who converted Josaphat.[10]

The tradition behind Fulgentius' ideas on the true meaning of the *Aeneid* and the myths he examined in his *Mitologiarum*, together with the high opinion men like Lactantius held of pagan insight, opened the way to a more sophisticated adaptation of pagan material. This adaptive technique is of course everywhere apparent in early Christian culture: in the transmutation of pagan festivals and deities, in the taming of pagan artistic motifs in the Book of Kells and the great Anglo-Saxon gospels, and in the patristic writers' fondness for quoting and bending the words of pre-Christian thinkers. A properly religious purpose could justify the preservation of pagan material— to lure men into church, as Aldhelm did with his secular songs, or to dramatize, ornament, or illustrate matters of doctrine. Thus Jerome (taught by Donatus, allegorizer of Virgil) recommended treating pagan works in the way Deuteronomy recommends that the Israelite treat a foreign wife, cutting off hair and nails so that the beauty should not seduce but should serve God. His arguments—this and others—were used in defense of pagan writers throughout the Middle Ages.

The Christian adaptation of pagan stories was at times quite superficial, as in the case of the Irish *Siabur-Charpat Culaind* (*The Demoniac Chariot of Cuchullain*),[11] which seems to date from the eighth century or earlier. The poem deals with St. Patrick's calling of Cuchullain from the dead at the request of doubting King Laoghaire. Cuchullain exhorts Laoghaire to become a Christian, and when

Laoghaire doubts Cuchullain's identity, Cuchullain convinces him by reciting his earthly deeds. Laoghaire accepts conversion, and Patrick says that heaven awaits Cuchullain. Here Christianity is simply the frame and pretended *raison d'être* for a group of old stories of Cuchullain's exploits.

Allegory provided a more sophisticated means of adaptation. An early example is Synesius' *Ægyptus sive de Providentia,* in which the good Osiris and the wicked Typhon, representing rival political figures of Synesius' time, struggle for control and provide the dramatic framework for a philosophical exploration of God's permission of evil. Another early example is the obscure pseudo-Lactantian *Phoenix,* a work which was to be further expanded and allegorized by a poet of the Cynewulfian school. The same method of course informs the tradition leading to the Old English *Physiologus.* The most ingenious adaptive use of older material, however, is that which we find in the Old English *Seafarer* and, at the peak of the tradition, *Beowulf.* A comparison of the *Seafarer* and analogous Old Welsh elegiac verse[12] suggests that the basis of the Anglo-Saxon poem may have been a literal and secular elegiac poem which the Christian poet has reshaped to create his literal-allegorical journey to the only lasting security for human "seafarers." The technique, if present (let us simply assume for the moment that it is), marks a striking advance from that of the *Physiologus,* the *Phoenix,* and the like. Here the allegory is not appended to literal material but is inherent in it, established by ambiguities and spiritual reverberations in the literal material itself.[13] At this stage in the evolution of poetic style, the poetic motivation is obviously not simply the preservation of old stories, nor is it the preacher's delight in lively illustration. Like the Old Saxon *Heliand,* the Old Saxon and Old English translations of Genesis, the German versions of such stories as that of Christ and the Woman of Samaria, and the *Evangelienbuch* of Otfried of Weissenburg, such adaptive allegories as *Beowulf* and the *Seafarer* assume an audience sophisticated in orthodox theology and present themselves as self-conscious demonstrations that the native language—and now even native stories —can give sublime expression to learned material. Just as Otfried's work was aimed, as W. T. H. Jackson says, "not at a general lay public, which could not possibly have understood it, but at the small group of people who, although already educated in Latin, spoke German as a native tongue,[14] so *Beowulf* and the *Seafarer* were aimed at highly educated Christian Anglo-Saxons. They are works conspicuous for their pride in the native heritage and for their conviction that native experience and legend might as readily be allegorized as anything from pagan Greece or Rome.

From this technique, Anglo-Saxon poetry moved a step further in the poetry of Cynewulf. What the *Seafarer-, Wanderer-,* and *Beowulf-* poets did with old pagan or secular materials, Cynewulf would do with Christian subject matter. In *Elene,* as we shall see, he transforms a literal saint's life to create a literal-allegorical poem on salvation, in which characters and events are at once historical and typic. In the *Dream of the Rood* he or some follower allegorizes the crucifixion itself.

As this brief survey should suggest, Anglo-Saxon poetry evolved along lines visible on the Continent as well. Thanks to its late start, perhaps, or perhaps thanks to that pride in tradition and ancestry so evident in Anglo-Saxon culture, poetry in Old English escapes the evolutionary stage represented by Prudentius, in which Christian poetry was essentially polemic. Indeed, the number of pagan and secular poems preserved in Old English would seem to indicate that, despite their occasional complaints against things pagan, Englishmen came to Christianity late enough to escape some of the hostility common in a new religion's attitude to its predecessor. Caedmon's *Hymn,* one of the oldest of the poems surviving in Old English, shows an adaptation of traditional style and Christian content (if the usual view of the poem's heroic diction is right)[15] so perfect and so comfortable that one cannot help finding the poem— as Bede did—"miraculous." Both in general nature (as biblical "translation") and in its techniques of organization and development, Caedmonic poetry is roughly analogous to the poetry of Juvencus, Sedulius, Avitus, and others, but it comes at the peak of its tradition and in general escapes the tradition's false starts. The second phase of Anglo-Saxon poetic evolution, in which older material is turned to Christian use either in relatively simple or in complex fashion, as in the *Physiologus* and *Beowulf,* respectively, has again its continental background of theory and practice. The final, Cynewulfian phase has German antecedents but remains largely an English invention.

There can be little doubt that Anglo-Saxon poetry derived from two rhetorical traditions, one native, one classical. If there were no well-defined native poetic (however scops learned it), we would be hard put to explain the obvious degeneration of meter, of kenning-formation, and of other devices in late Anglo-Saxon poetry. Clearly Caedmon, Caedmon's early imitators, and such men as the *Beowulf-*

poet knew something which, with the passing of time, was lost or, at any rate, transformed. As for the scops' knowledge of some classical rhetorical theory—theory impossible to impose on, say, the poetic remains in Old Norse—the only evidence is the construction of the poems.

Classical rhetoric, as preserved by medieval rhetoricians accessible in Anglo-Saxon England, divided the process of composition into three stages, which can be described (somewhat over-simply) as: *inventio,* the choice of material and subject matter; *dispositio,* the arrangement of materials chosen; and *elocutio* (or *amplificatio*), the development of this material. (The two further elements of rhetorical theory, *memoria* and *pronuntiatio,* are not relevant to poetic composition.) The theoreticians known to the Anglo-Saxons devote little space to the third stage of composition, development. Not until the twelfth century and after, in the works of such writers as Matthieu de Vendôme, Geoffroi de Vinsauf, and Évrard l'Allemand, does rhetorical ornamentation overshadow all other concerns. As scholars have frequently pointed out, Martianus Capella, a typical early case, devotes to *inventio* and *dispositio* more than twice the space he grants to *elocutio*—proportions to be reversed by later writers.

Again brief review of familiar matter will be useful:

Inventio normally means not the creation of new plots, illustrations, and the like, but a selection of thesis and a choice of old materials which can be brought together in support of the thesis. As a servant of oratory, *rhetorica* gives the narrative poet very little direct help at this stage of composition; nevertheless, as poets like Victor, Sedulius, Dracontius, and Avitus show, the principles of *inventio* could easily be transferred to poetic composition. Sedulius, for example, collects materials involving miraculous deliverance in Scripture; Dracontius, pursuing the theme of God's mercy, combines an account of his personal trials with biblical and pagan stories.

Dispositio involves two considerations: the arrangement of materials which is most logical and the arrangement which is likely to be most persuasive. These entail questions of tone and occasion, matters which influence the writer's choice of point of attack (beginning, middle, end), his choice of his way of beginning (with a proverb, a situation or example, and so forth), and his choice of placement of his various assembled materials, his outline. Once the writer has made these decisions—precisely the decisions the serious contemporary novelist must make—he turns to development of his material, amplifying, abbreviating, and ornamenting what he has selected and arranged. It will be sufficient for the moment merely to mention a few of the prescribed techniques. The writer may amplify through explanatory phrases, the evasion of direct statement, through simile or metaphor, apostrophe, personification, the introduction of new but parallel material, affirmation after negation, and so on. He may shorten by merely summarizing his source, by joining two events or ideas into one, by putting a variety of things under one general heading, by giving merely the general sense of involved ideas, and so on. For ornamentation, the rhetoric books give the writer various tropes, figures of diction, and such "figures of thought" as understatement, comparison, vivid description, dialogue, ambiguity, and hyperbole.[16]

What matters for the moment is simply this: the lore of classical and early medieval rhetoricians was available to educated Anglo-Saxon poets, and the considerable learning of those poets in other areas gives weight to the hypothesis that their style adapted the rhetorical techniques of the learned. In some cases—for example, the *Seafarer*—we have fair evidence that a Christian poet consciously adapted an earlier elegiac form to an allegorical purpose. We have clear evidence, in some cases, that the Anglo-Saxon poet could make free use of diverse sources for a unified effect. Cynewulf's well-known interweaving of source materials is the most obvious example; but Bonjour's explication of the so-called digressions in *Beowulf*[17] showed long ago that the *Beowulf*-poet used an equally self-conscious method. It cannot be shown that the technique of combining old materials for a new purpose does not come from oral tradition rather than from the rhetoric books. Hrothgar's scop, no student of Latin, works by juxtaposing old stories with new to praise Beowulf; and *Deor,* too, appears to combine fragmentary *thulas* and bits of gnomic verse for a new purpose, apparently a bid for patronage.[18] Despite their generally recognized errors of premise and execution, the studies of Müllenhoff, ten Brink, and others have made it clear that poems like *Beowulf* may have been composed by a traditional method of adapting, expanding, and modifying older lays to construct an epic whole[19]—a poetic method possibly untouched by classical *rhetorica.* But as we learn by comparison of surviving Germanic short lays (*Finnsburg, Hildebrand*) and epic use of the same material, lays and their epic parallels differ fundamentally in complexity and scale. Since we have from ancient Germania no such poems as the *Iliad,* the *Odyssey,* or the *Gilgamesh,* where a traditional method of legend combination is evident—since we have, in fact, only poems in which the assembly of diverse materials might be either the product of a hypothetical pre-Christian Germanic

poetic method or the product of classical rhetorical theory as transmitted by Christian writers—it is impossible to say whether the method
found in *Beowulf* or *Genesis* is classical, native, or something of both.
(Common sense says, "both.")

Nearly every question we ask concerning traditional Germanic
poetic theory leaves us equally frustrated. We may perhaps hope for
eventual scholarly agreement on the early Anglo-Saxon poet's metrical
theory; but as any first-rate poet will tell you, and as discussions
since Pope's famous study suggest, no fully acceptable—no even re-
motely acceptable—theory has so far been devised. We are on equally
uncertain ground when we consider, in A. C. Bartlett's phrase, "the
larger rhetorical patterns."[20] No one doubts that the patterns exist;
the question yet to be answered is, are the patterns uniquely Anglo-
Saxon? We are on safer ground—but not much safer—when we turn
to syntax, verbal style, and the oral formulaic character of Old English
poetry.[21] Suffice it to say, for now, that a traditional Germanic poetic
did provide scops with specific techniques for circumlocution, sentence
order, reference control, and so forth, though even in such matters as
diction convention, things are not always as clear as we might wish.

We are often very uncertain, then, of which of the two available
traditions of rhetoric is at work in a given poem or line. The problem
increases in complexity if we consider Celtic tradition as well. In
analyzing the style of particular poems we have therefore no choice
but to focus on the exact way in which each poem seems to be constructed, discovering its principles from within. This has long been
the usual method of those who have studied Anglo-Saxon poetry. But
by keeping both classical rhetorical principles and standard native
practice in mind, as a check *afterward* on theories worked out from
inside the poems, and by resisting interpretive hypotheses not likely
within either of those two traditions, we gain for our interpretations a
measure of historical probability. Where neither tradition gives us
clues, we must depend on critical judgment and on what we know of
the nature of poetic meaning in general—that is, the nature of statement and innuendo; of, in the old sense, allegory.

Allegory

In the end, of course, one does not discover the meaning of a poem
by studying the rhetorical tradition behind it; the rhetorical tradition
merely suggests approaches and gives support to interpretations
reached through analysis of the poem itself. Both for this reason and

because we sometimes cannot tell which rhetorical tradition informs a given poem, it will be useful to set down here a few universal principles governing poetic signaling in any rhetorical tradition.

The first principle is that all poetry tends toward *allegory* in the ancient sense—*allos* + *agoreuein;* in other words, all poetry tends to be speech other than that of the assembly or marketplace. It suggests more than it states, and, in large measure, its suggestion is controlled. The list in a telephone book is pure statement: what it means by definition and common consent. A newspaper account may suggest more than it says, but the level of control is low: the account of a murder may suggest, say, ethical principles to the reader, but if the account is strictly a piece of reporting, the writer is either indifferent to the suggestion or is slyly turning his genre into one more sophisticated. In historical writing, fiction, and so forth, the level of controlled suggestion is high; by stylistic means, the writer makes his suggestion clear—even if he does not fully understand what he is suggesting. For instance, if a novelist speaks, at several points in his narrative, of the mountains looming above his characters, the reiteration implies some meaning in the image. Whether the writer has a conscious purpose (e.g., mountains as signs of the littleness of man) or no conscious purpose, merely an unexamined nervous feeling about mountains, the image implies something, and the reader is teased toward a meaning beyond that which is stated. With or without the writer's approval, the mountains have become what Aristotle calls a *kosmos*—a significant ornament or, loosely, symbol.[22] Suggestion is controlled, then, when by formal means within the work the writer shows what things are somehow significant and what things not.

Despite efforts to revive it, the word *allegory* is admittedly a troublesome critical term, even in technical discussions of, for instance, Gregory or Fulgentius. It has become so debased, in some quarters, and its application has become so haphazard, that its main function now may be to annoy people predisposed to dislike patristic exegesis or win the hearts of people convinced that all medieval literature is disguised Christian meditation. Yet the recent revival of the word is right, since no other quite works. Let *allegory* be understood here as shorthand for the idea that poetry is the most suggestive of all forms of literature, enforcing its suggestions by a greater distortion of natural speech than any other genre can afford. (When prose achieves a similar degree of distortion—as in *Finnegans Wake*—we call it prose poetry.)

The second general principle of poetic signaling is that what I have called "suggestion" is always stylistic; that is, it is the result of formal elements of style which can be isolated and defined. These elements appear to fall into four classes: Aristotle's *kosmoi,* rhythmic encoding, syntactic implication, and structural implication.

As Aristotle uses the word, a *kosmos* is an ornament—a word, or in an extended sense, an image, scene, rhetorical flight, etc., which by its nature stands out from its background, like an ornament on a Christmas tree, capturing attention. Angus Fletcher, who would like to revive the word, describes a *kosmos* as "any decoration or ornament of dress, any embellishment, any costume particularly denoting status, any heraldic device that might accompany the donning of such a costume. . . ."[23] Tramps' shoes, like crowns, are "cosmic." A *kosmos* may in fact be any striking detail—Achilles' shield, the burning lake, or the character Grendel in *Beowulf,* a sudden shift in diction, or a literary allusion which makes a particular passage stand out, isolated yet implicitly relevant to the poetic whole. To revive the word may be to introduce confusion ("The cross in the *Dream of the Rood* is a 'cosmic' image"); but modern alternatives are hard to come by. *Ornament* implies mere decoration. *Symbol* implies consistent symbolic structure. And such words as *emblem* and *hieroglyph* are even more confusing. A *kosmos,* then, is any discrete element in a poem—image, character, or rhetorical flourish—which by its nature, that is, its "charge" or, as Aristotle says, its "aliveness," tells us there is something to be noticed or unlocked. The identification of poetic *kosmoi* need not be subjective. Whenever the poet dwells on some particular event, character, or image, whenever he introduces unusual stylistic devices, whenever he in any way calls special attention to something in his story, he is wittingly or unwittingly presenting a key detail. Thus, for example, the following lines from *Beowulf* are stylistically unusual within the poem and must be recognized as *kosmic:*

> Nu is þines mægnes blæd
> ane hwile;   eft sona bið,
> þæt þec adl oððe ecg   eafoþes getwæfeð,
> *oððe* fyres feng,   *oððe* flodes wylm,
> *oððe* gripe meces,   *oððe* gares fliht,
> *oððe* atol yldo;   *oððe* eagena bearhtm
> forsiteð ond forsworceð;   semninga bið,
> þaet ðec, dryhtguma,   deað oferswyðeð.
>
> (*Beowulf,* 1761b–68; my italics)

By *rhythmic encoding,* the second class of signaling devices (the phrase is Fletcher's), I mean any form of stylistic or structural repetition which, like an isolated *kosmos,* catches the reader's attention and prompts him to ask himself what the point is, or, in this case, what the connection between the disturbed details may be. Chaucer's *Book of the Duchess* (like Cynewulf's *Christ*) is a tour de force of rhythmic encoding.[24] The narrator in Chaucer's poem discovers a gardenlike place and says of it,

> . . . hit was, on to beholde,
> As thogh the erthe envye wolde
> To be gayer than the heven,
> To have mo floures, swiche seven
> As in the welken sterres be.
> Hit had forgete the povertee
> That winter, through his colde morwes,
> Had mad hit suffren, and his sorwes.

(405–12)

Later, the Knight in the poem says of his lady:

> For I dar swere, withoute doute,
> That as the someres sonne bright
> Is fairer, clerer, and hath more light
> Than any [other] planete in heven,
> The mone, or the sterres seven,
> For al the worlde, so had she
> Surmounted hem alle of beaute. . . .

(820–26)

Standing alone, the garden image functions as a *kosmos* (in this instance, a conventional one); but when details from the description of the garden are reintroduced in association with the lady, the two descriptions together become the outward sign or code for the poet's suggestion—here a suggestion that the lady and the world are equivalent, and that earthly beauty must fade.

Fletcher explains rhythmic encoding as follows: "If one wanted to establish a code using a series of unfamiliar signals, let us say bell sounds of different pitches instead of dots and dashes, one would have to repeat certain key combinations in a sort of ritual. The listener who picked up the repeated sounds would at first see no message in them, but gradually would perceive the repetitive pattern, an imposed 'code,' and would try deciphering what he heard."[25] Poems are codes in this sense. Using language, not bells, the poet who wishes both to suggest more than he says openly and to control his suggestion must somehow provide clues. If the poem's surface is enigmatic (as in the *Book of the Duchess*), we know the poem not random and accidental because we catch the periodic repetitions. If the surface seems quite plain and direct, but arbitrary, while formal devices are not arbitrary but seem to develop by some secret law, we know we must search beyond the surface statement. *The Fates of the Apostles,* as James Boren has shown, is a case in point.[26] The surface presents a rambling catalogue, but the "rings," the system of regularly falling three-word clusters, indicate some poetic purpose beyond the surface statement. Rhythmic encoding need not always be verbal, of course. Parallel images, even events (Beowulf's three monster fights, for instance) may provide the cipher. Needless to say, not all repetition is significant: some verbal or structural rhythms are matters of frozen convention. The critic must distinguish between the reiterated phrase *wordum ond worcum* in Beowulf, a phrase which is "marked," or thematically significant, and *Beowulf maþelode, bearn Ecgþeowes,* which is not.

A third form of stylistic signaling is what I have called *syntactic implication.* This occurs whenever syntax raises questions which cannot be answered on the syntactic level. In Anglo-Saxon this most often happens in the figure *parataxis* (nonsubordination: *he ran and she walked*). In the *Dream of the Rood,* for example, the poet says, "Syllic waes se sigebeam, ond ic synnum fah . . ."(13). The absence of any subordination raises the question: What is the dreamer's relationship to the apparent subject of the poem, the cross? Or, to put it another way: in a passage ostensibly devoted to description of the cross, why is the dreamer introduced as (in terms of syntax) an equal?

Structural implication is another signaling device. It arises whenever we find, in the structural development of a poem, some seeming mistake of juxtaposition or symmetry, an apparent *non sequitur.* For example, in the *Fates of the Apostles* we find a regular progression of persecution agents—those who bring apostles to their fates—and then, unexpectedly, in the slot reserved for the persecution agent, we find Christ. The reader is forced toward an unstated connection between Fate and Providence, a connection which informs the remainder of the poem. Later, in the syntactic slot reserved for the apostle we find the poet (as Everyman). Again, structure implies meaning. A rather different instance of structural implication may be found in *Beowulf,* at lines 183b–87:

> Wa bið þæm ðe sceal
> þurh sliðne nið   sawle bescufan

in fyres fæþm,   frofre ne wenan,
wihte gewendan!   Wel bið þæm þe mot
æfter deaðdæge   Drihten secean. . . .

At first glance, the moralizing aside seems to appear without background: one cannot make out what prompted it. When the reader re-examines the passage leading up to the aside, he sees the situations of Grendel and Hrothgar in a new way, one which makes the aside something other than whimsey. Grendel is like a sinner in the Christian framework; Hrothgar is a pagan prefiguration of the Christian faithful man.

If poetic suggestion is always stylistic, consisting of formal elements of style which can be isolated and defined, then the interpretation of poetry is in large measure nonsubjective. That may be an offensive opinion to some readers, but it is true, at least up to a point. It is the premise of classical (and exegetical) rhetoric, which from Aristotle's time forward sought to categorize the ways in which subtle meaning is communicated. Good poetry, from a strictly formal point of view, is that which, once its stylistic suggestions have all been identified and understood, makes coherent sense. Bad poetry is that which sends out accidental signals and ends in confusion. The only reservation common sense would insist on, here, is that sometimes evidence in a very short poem is, however consistent, insufficient to prove the poem not a lucky accident. Classical rhetoric is essentially descriptive, and insofar as it describes correctly what happens in the poetic process, it should apply to any poetry. As for the native Germanic poetic, it may or may not have been theoretical in the same way; but the scop who used it must have been concerned with predictable achievement of the same ends that Greek poets sought—illumination (or "instruction") and delight.

The investigation of particular poems in Old English need not take either Latin or hypothetical Germanic poetic as its premise: by study of *kosmoi,* rhythmic encoding, etc., one can work out meaning by internal analysis. The underlying rhetoric, as I have said, provides only historical probability for the reading. But consideration of the poem's apparent rhetorical premises does become important when one turns from study of individual poems to study of the stylistic relationships among several poems in the tradition—one concern of this book. To know specific ways in which Caedmonic, Christian elegiac, and Cynewulfian poetry are similar in their rhetoric is to know something about Anglo-Saxon Christian poetic style in general, that is, to know ways in which Anglo-Saxon poetry differs from the poetry of other times and places, and ways in which it must have differed from Anglo-Saxon "plain speech." To know the central rhetorical devices (both type and frequency) which distinguish Caedmonic from Cynewulfian poetry is to begin to understand the Caedmonic and Cynewulfian styles.

2

Caedmonic Poetry

The central problem for the critic dealing with Caedmonic (or "Caedmonian") poetry has been that of sorting out native Teutonic elements from Christian and discovering the relationship between the two. For some critics, it is the fusing of the two traditions that makes the miracle Bede felt to be present in Caedmon's *Hymn*.[1] If one deals with the *Hymn* alone—the only authentic work of Caedmon—the problem takes these forms: Did Caedmon create new vocabulary and new formulas or did he (as Magoun thinks) use formulas which had slowly developed and had been used in Caedmon's presence many times?[2] Did his vocabulary and formulas come from the psalms, not from native tradition at all?[3] Does the *Hymn* show knowledge of sophisticated Latin rhetorical theory?[4] The answers to all these questions is a doubtful "perhaps." The poem is structurally, as well as metrically, brilliant, as B. F. Huppé has shown most convincingly.[5] But the poem is only nine lines long, which means that no cumulative structural or textural proofs are possible, and it is connected with a legend of an untutored cowherd. It can be shown that the hymn lacks the padding and occasional clumsiness of, say, the metrical Psalms,[6] but its positive virtues, especially its seemingly sophisticated structure, must be left to individual assessment.

Longer poems in the Caedmonic school—even those which are strikingly inferior to Caedmon's *Hymn*—provide a better basis for analysis of Caedmonic style. The poems, one finds, are remarkably similar in rhetorical method. We will consider two representative examples, *Genesis* and *Daniel,* and a third poem, *Christ and Satan,* which, though in some respects Caedmonic, is close enough to the style of Cynewulf to provide a stylistic contrast.

Genesis A

Until recently, scholars have regularly viewed *Genesis A* and *B*[7] strictly in terms of the Teutonicizing of the biblical story by means of Germanic poetic formulas and cultural premises. B. F. Huppé has presented a new reading which minimizes Teutonic qualities and finds *Genesis* a tightly constructed spiritual-symbolic work meant to be read in Christian exegetical fashion.[8]

Huppé's reading may be right, up to a point, though forced; but it does not overthrow the older view.[9] Whether or not the poet's audience was "clerical," as Huppé believes, the poet obviously pictured Old Testament life—especially in time of war—in the images familiar to a northerner and saw Old Testament virtues in an Anglo-Saxon way. Professor Greenfield comments that "the thematic pattern perceived in *Genesis A* [by Huppé] seems quite a lucid account of that poem's coherence," but adds that "many of the 'spiritual' meanings need no specific exegetical knowledge to fathom, but are rather naturally inherent in the narrative material; Cain's slaying of Abel, for example, as symbolizing 'the results of the Fall—man's self-willed sinning,' or the fall of Sodom and Gomorrah as symbolizing 'both salvation, in Lot's escape, and damnation, in the destruction of the city and in the fate of Lot's wife.' "[10] Greenfield cites two short battle passages (1989–93b and 2061–67a) which obviously have far more to do with Germania than with Christian *caritas.*

It should be evident at a glance that if *Genesis A* is in some sense allegorical, it is not sophisticated and original allegorical "translation" of the kind we find in, for example, the Middle English *Purity.*[11] In dealing with the possibility of allegory in *Genesis A,* then, the critic must ask two questions, the second more important than the first, though dependent upon it. (1) How well does the tradition of scriptural exegesis apply to the Old Testament events recounted in the poem? and (2) How can one know that any allegory discovered in the poem belongs specifically to the poem, not merely to the source? Huppé has dealt with the first question. Stylistic analysis must deal with the second.

It is true enough that the Anglo-Saxon poem is no mere paraphrase.

The Old Testament narrative is in some places shortened, in others amplified as we would expect it to be under the hypothesis that the poem was composed according to exegetical principles of *translatio*. Though much of the poem must be set down as hackwork (the drab genealogies, the inevitable carpenter's specifications for the Ark, etc.), the poem does have, even in its duller moments, rhetorical design. The translation is not necessarily complete, and even what we call *Genesis A* may not be the work of a single hand; nevertheless, the poem is orderly in that certain ideas, images, and words are systematically emphasized.

As all scholars but Huppé have agreed, the Teutonicizing of the Old Testament story is the most striking thing about the poem. It is in fact the poem's rhetorical and thematic premise, governing both the poet's choice of specific phrases ("þegnas þrymfæste," used of angels) and his choice of ideas and events to be elaborated as keys to meaning.

The theme of the poem, announced at the outset, is that it is fitting, "riht micel," that men should praise and love God (or loyally serve him—*lufian*) because of his power ("He is mægna sped," 3) and because he is eternal (5b ff.). Failure to serve God is presented throughout the poem as foolishness or madness, a failure of *ræd* (24, and see discussion of *ræd*, below). The grounds of this fitting love and service, however doctrinal, are insistently Germanic: Men and angels are God's *comitatus*, and the requirements of loyalty are two—love of the chieftain (God) and faithfulness to kinsmen. Right service of God means, in effect, meadhall-joy: What God gives is *ræd, eðel, sinc*, and (treated as a form of treasure) lineage. Disloyalty leads to the traditional sorrows of the exile. Safety under God's protection and misery in exile from God form the central contrast in the poem and account for the selection of detail in every episode. Diction carries the metaphor:

> Heagum þrymmum
> soðfæst and swiðfeorm   sweglbosmas heold,
> þa wæron gesette   wide and side
> þurh geweald goes   wuldres bearnum,
> gasta weardum.   Hæfdon gleam and dream,
> and heora ordfruman,   engla þreatas,
> beorhte blisse.   Wæs heora blæd micel!
>   Þegnas þrymfæste   eoden heredon,
> sægdon lustum lof,   heora liffrean
> demdon, drihtenes   dugeþum wæron
> swiðe gesælige.
>
>   (8b–18a)

Whereas God's loyal thanes are "gesette wide and side" and enjoy "gleam and dream," and "blæd micel," standard formulas for meadhall joys or the comforts of a secure kingdom, the disloyal angels get an exile's home (*wræclicne ham*, 37a). Their crime is thoroughly Teutonicized: They turn from kinsman-love "for oferhygde" (22b) and make war-boasts (e.g., 25b). The poet's treatment of God's reaction to their disloyalty is also typically Germanic: they get an ironic "reward" —*leane* (37b), an irony paralleled in *Beowulf* (114b). The false angels' defeat and exile is now elaborated (28b–77) and followed by a contrasting image of the loyal angels' joy. Whereas the place of the fallen angels is "dreamaleas" (40a), God having dealt with them as would a powerful Anglo-Saxon warrior (60b–64), those still in heaven are joyfully secure:

> Þa wæs soð swa ær   sibb on heofnum,
> fægre freoþoþeawas,   frea eallum leof,
> þeoden his þegnum;   þrymmas weoxon
> duguða mid drihtne,   dreamhæbbendra.
>
> (78–81)

The same contrast between the joys of loyal thanes and the sorrows of the exile informs every major episode in *Genesis A*. In their unfallen state, Adam and Eve, like the loyal angels, are joyful (even during the removal of his rib, Adam "sar ne wiste"—179b—a detail surely introduced for the sake of thematic design). When they fall, the poet emphasizes the sorrows they must endure as exiles. In the Cain and Abel story the poet focuses on Cain's exile: ". . . þu flema scealt/eidlast wrecan, winemagum lað" (1020b–21), and,

> Heht þa from hweorfan
> meder and magum   manscyldigne,
> cnosle sinum.   Him þa Cain gewat
> gongan geomormod   gode of gesyhðe,
> wineleas wrecca. . . .
>
> (1047–51a)

At one point in the Abraham story the poet underscores (and Christianizes) his exile motif by commenting on the relative unimportance of the loss of one's earthly lord if one still has God, the heavenly chieftain:

> næfre hleowlora
> æt edwihtan   æfre weorðeð

feorhberendra   forht and acol,
mon for Metode,   þe him æfter a
þurh gemynda sped   mode and dædum,
worde and gewitte,   wise þance,
oð his ealdorgedal   oleccan wile.

(1953b–59)

(The poet of course repeatedly contrasts the power of God and that of earthly kings.) The poet again and again expands his source to give dramatic force to the idea of exile—in the story of Hagar (2264b ff.), in the threat against Lot (2480 ff.), and at various incidental points in the narrative (e.g., 2819 ff.). Even Abraham's trip with Isaac to Mt. Moriah has overtones of the exile motif, if we pay close attention to diction:

          Þa he fus gewat
from his agenum hofe   Isaac lædan,
bearn unweaxen,   swa him bebead Metod.
Efste þa swiðe   and onette
forð foldwege,   swa him Frea tæhte
wegas ofer westen. . . .

(2870–75a; my italics)

The exile motif reflects the negative side of the poet's image of God as Teutonic chieftain. On the positive side, God wins battles, deals out treasures to those who have earned them, gives his thanes a safe place to live, and so forth. The poem's first episode shows God trouncing the devil:

          Þa he gebolgen wearð,
besloh synsceaþan   sigore and gewealde,
dome and dugeðe,   and dreame benam
his feond, friðo   and gefean ealle,
torhte tire,   and his torn gewræc
on gesacum swiðe   selfes mihtum
strengum stiepe.   Hæfde styrne mod,
gegremed grymme,   grap on wraðe
faum folmum,   and him on fæðm gebræc
yrre on mode. . . .

(54b–63a)

It is this military power of God, always presented largely in stock Germanic formulas and often involving the visually concrete word *grap*, that makes God's human thanes invincible and, combined with his wisdom, makes God praiseworthy. The point is most explicit in the Abraham section, when Abraham's small force, aided by God, overcomes a huge force (to the usual music of weapons and ravens). The victory is a strictly materialistic and Anglo-Saxon sort of thing:

> Hlyn wearð on vicum
> scylda and sceafta,   sceotendra fyll,
> guðflana gegrind;   gripon unfægre
> under sceat werum   scearpe garas,
> and feonda feorh   feollon ðicce,
> þær hlihende   huðe feredon
> secgas and gesiððas.
>
> (2061b–67a)

The laughter of booty-grabbers here is obviously a Teutonic detail. But though the point in this passage is that God can overwhelm enemies and take their treasures, the earthly treasures are not, for the Christian poet, the important thing. When Melchisedech and his lord, "guðcyning, Sodoma aldor," come to Abraham to bemoan the loss of their treasures and women, now recaptured by Abraham and his allies, Abraham somewhat reluctantly gives them his share of the recaptured booty—"wunden gold," "feoh and frætwa" (2128–30). God asserts his value as a guardian despite Abraham's apparent loss of goods (2168–72), and when Abraham asks what it is that God gives him, "freomanna to frofre, nu ic þus feasceaft eom" (2176), God promises a son who will "keep the treasures" (2190) as a Teutonic prince would do, and promises also a line of kinsmen, metaphoric treasure, who will fill the earth as the jewellike stars (2191b–92a) "woldorfæstne wlite wide dælað" (2193). (Note in passing the choice of *dælað*, not for alliteration.)

Though most explicit in this passage, the motif of God's military and more-than-military power appears in each major episode—in his establishment of the kingdom of heaven, Eden, Canaan, etc., in his placing at Eden's gates an armed angelic sentry whom no man's might can overcome (948–51), and in his victories over the disloyal angels, the evildoers of Noah's generation, the Sodomites who misuse his messengers, and so forth. In each case, God founds a kingdom and gives laws ("Go multiply; slay no kinsmen"), and those who obey his laws prosper, whereas those who do not are exiled into darkness or death. The structural justification of the tedious genealogies, aside from Germanic delight in *thula*, is partly that they show man's obedience to the command, "Multiply," given to Adam and again to Noah, but mainly that they show God's kingly generosity to his loyal thanes. Until Abraham pleads for Abimelech, God's anger toward that king makes Abimelech's race barren (2742 ff.). The lineage motif is always Teutonicized. Those who marry wrongly, as in Noah's generation, are king- or kinsman-betrayers (1248–84).

Loyalty, we have said, means knowing one's place in relation to chieftain and kinsmen, whether in the metaphysical kingdom or in the individual household; disloyalty lies in the rejection of one's place or harm of a kinsman. Take the cases of Hagar and Ishmael. Like the disloyal angels and like Adam and Eve, Hagar is proud:

> Ongan æfþancum   agendfrean
> halsfæst herian,   higeþryðe wæg,
> wæs laðwendo,   lustum ne wolde
> þeowdom þolian,   ac heo þriste ongan
> wið Sarran swiðe winnan.

> (2239–43)

Because of Hagar's pride, Sarah scolds her and she flees to exile: "on sið gewat/westen secan" (2267b–68a). An angel of God stops Hagar, reminds her that she is owned by Sarah, and makes her a promise, parallel to God's promise to Abraham, that her race will be numberless —but a race descended from a man dedicated, like Cain, to darkness and evil (2289–92). The angel charges Hagar to accept her lawful place ("wuna þæm þe agon!"—2295b), and she, obedient now, returns home and accepts her position as servant. When she is exiled by Abraham later it is not for her pride but because her son, illegitimate and, we have heard, "orlæggifre" (2289b), is a threat to Isaac's rightful heritage: Ishmael would usurp Isaac's place, harming his brother (2788 ff). Abraham, who loves Hagar as God loved Adam, asks that the exile be tempered, and God gives exile but ultimate glory.

As I have tried to suggest in my summary of it, the Hagar-Ishmael story has numerous parallels with other events in the poem. The clue to the parallels (Hagar-Satan, Hagar-Adam and Eve, Ishmael-Cain) lies, we will discover, in the poet's allegorical treatment of heaven, Eden, and earthly paradises like Sodom. At the locking of Eden, the poet says:

> ne mæg ær inwitfull   ænig gaferan
> womscyldig mon,   ac se weard hafað
> miht and strengðo,   se þet mære lif
> dugeðum deore   drihtne healdeð.

> (948–51)

No guilty man may occupy the place—no man guilty of pride, like Satan, Adam and Eve, or Hagar, or guilty of the betrayal of kinsmen, like Cain, like those who turn to the daughters of Cain, or like Ishmael. The implication is that when guilt is removed, Eden, type of heaven, may be approached.

In contrast to those who are disloyal to their earthly or heavenly king the poet presents figures of loyalty, among them Noah (1285–86a), the two sons of Noah who show respect for their father, avoiding the disloyalty of Cam (1580 ff.), and Abraham. In contrast to those who harm kinsmen the poet presents figures of *siblufan,* among them Noah, whom God compliments for his never having been "to broðor banan" (1526a), and Abraham, who courageously rescues Lot despite bad odds. Though the conclusion of the poem we have may not have been the poet's intended conclusion, it is thematically striking, since Abraham's willingness to sacrifice his son for his chieftain brings the two Teutonic laws together.

In support of this general description of the poem's rhetorical design, one can offer two kinds of concrete evidence—first, structural analysis, which breaks the poem down into rhetorical units and notes the rhetorically emphatic details (those underscored by *repetitio, interpretatio,* etc.), and second, textural analysis, that is, examination of images and locutions insistently repeated throughout the poem. Structurally, the poem can be outlined as follows:

I. God and Lucifer

1–8a. The rightness of praising and loving God for his eternal power as king "ofer heofenstolas" (8a).

8b–21. The joy and virtue of angels who love and obey (16–18a) their Lord.

21–77. God's suppression and exile of the disloyal angels, depriving them of joy.

78–91. The joy of the loyal angels, at peace (78b) and at *one* (82a), blessed with *duguða* and *dream* (81), on contrast to those "leohte belorene" (86a).

II. Adam and Eve

92–112. God's decision to make a new kingdom, earth, by bringing light and order to darkness and waste (104 ff.).

112–68a. Creation of the world, with emphasis on angels' eager obedience of God (121b ff.), God's removal of darkness (117–22b, 127b, 128a, 133b, 134a, etc.), and God's great power (passim).

169–234. God's gifts to Adam—viz., Eve, lordship over Nature, the Kingdom of Eden (206 ff.)—with emphasis on the couple's joy while "ac him drihtnes wæs/bam on breostum byrnende lufu (190b–91).

234–851. Genesis B interpolated (to be examined later).

852–902. The Fall, resulting in the couple's sorrow and retreat to darkness (857–60a, etc.); their shame over nakedness; the serpent's guilt (897–902).

903–65. God's exile and curse of the snake (906–17); God's exile (919a) and curse of Eve (including her status as slave to man); the exile of Adam (oðerne eðel secean,/wynleasran wic, and on wræc hweorfan" [927–28]). The emphasis is on God's power, man's sorrow in exile.

III. Cain and Abel

965–86. Birth of Cain and Abel; Cain's sorrow ("torn were/hefig æt heortan," 279b–80a) at the angel's refusal to look at his offering (cf. exile's sorrow at removal from God); the murder.

987–1001. Authorial comment on the tree in Eden, cause of man's sorrow, its allegorical fruit ("of þam brad blado bealwa gehwilces/spryten ongunnon," 994–95a).

1002–54. Exile of Cain, God's prohibition of murder (kin-slaying), even of Cain. Emphasis on God's power, the exile's sorrow at loss of God's love and protection (1025 ff.) and at loss of fellowship of kinsmen (1047b ff.).

1055–1103. Cain's building of a hall and founding of a line; the murder of Cain (1093 ff.); the predicted sorrowful result of this kinsman-murder (1100–1103).

1104–27. In contrast to 1055–1103, God's kindness to Adam in replacing Abel with another son; Adam's death.

IV. The Flood

1128–1245a. Happiness and power of Seth's loyal kingdom and line, with emphasis (as in first episode) on light, bliss, joy (e.g., 1176–77a, 1197–1213, etc.).

1245b–84. Betrayal of God by Seth's kin (their love of his enemies); God's decision to punish truth-breakers as he punished Lucifer (cf. 1275–76a with 54b–64).

1285–1561. Noah and the Flood; emphasis on God's love and powerful protection of the loyal, whom he brings to "friŏ" (1299b) and life's greenness (1454a, 1458b, 1474a, etc.), in contrast to his destruction of the disloyal, who, though fair at the outset (e.g., 1252), come to darkness (1300b, 1301a, 1326a, 1355a, 1375a, 1379a, 1414a, etc.). The raven-dove story presents a contrast between the unfaithful raven (him seo wen geleah" 1446b) and the faithful dove who comes, like Noah, to life's greenness (1470) and, like Noah, gives an offering (1472).

1562–97. Noah's drunkenness; Ham's (Cam's) disloyal scorn; Noah's curse (parallel to God's curse of Eve) that he be "hean under heofnum, hleomago þeow" (1595; cf. 919b ff.).

1598–1654. Wealth and joy of Noah's loyal line of treasure-givers; their peacefulness and kin-love ("Folc wæs anmod" 1650b, cf. 1662a).

V. Babel

1655–1701. Founding of kingdom on Shinar plains—emphasis on greenness, beauty (1657b, 1658a) and on kinsmen's accord ("anmod," 1662a); building of the tower "for wlence and for wanhygdum" (1673); the confusion of tongues and sorrowful result, metaphoric exile: "æghwilc worden/mægburh fremde" (1694b–95a) and,

> Him on laste bu
> stiŏlic stantorr   and seo steape burh
> samod samworht   on Sennar stod.

(1699b–1701)

VI. Abraham

1702–1810. In contrast to those who, though loving kinsmen, were un-submissive to God, Abraham and Aaron love both God and kinsmen, and, in turn, "þam eorlum wæs/frea engla bam freond and aldor" (1710b–11). They prosper "on woruldrice" (1715 ff.); Abraham gets a beautiful wife, "fæger and freolic" (1722; cf. 1728a), as well as the promise of a beautiful kingdom (1750b–51), personal protection from harm (1752b ff.), and a great race (1762b). He goes to his bright and "ælgrene" new kingdom (1786 ff.) and gratefully gives thanks to God, "lifes leohtfruman (1792a ff.).

1811–72. Abraham among foreigners; his pretense that Sarah is his sister; God's wrath when the Pharaoh takes her to himself, and his demand that Abraham settle elsewhere.

1873–1920. Abraham's departure, building of a new kingdom, his offering of thanks, his refusal to allow trouble to develop between himself and Lot, his kinsman (1900b ff.).

1921–59. Lot settles in a seeming paradise, Sodom (1924a); his obedience to law (1943b) despite his neighbors (1935 ff.); Abraham's joy and security under God's powerful protection (1945–59).

1960–2095. The Elamites' sack of Sodom and capture of Lot; Abraham's rescue operation to save his kinsman. Emphasis on disloyalty of the enemy (cf. 1978–79), "ac him from swicon" (1981b), "norðmen wæron suðfolcum swice" (1995b–96a); loyalty and friendship or Abraham's allies and hearth-companions (2039b) to Abraham ("freondum sinum," 2025a; "fultumes wærfæst," 2025b–26a); enemies' brutal theft of women and treasure (1970a, 1972a, 2006b, 2007a, 2009b, 2010a, etc.). Final emphasis in this rhetorical unit (the authorial recapitulation) is on God's gift of power (2092b–95).

2096–2215. Abraham's generosity to Sodom's ruler; God's promised gift of lineage and kingdom, sources of joy:

> Ne geomra þu!
> Ic eom se waldend se þe for wintra fela
> of Caldea ceastre alædde,
> feowera sumne, gehet þe folcstede
> wide to gewealde.
>
> (2200b–2204a)

Cf. 2212 ff.

2216–2303. Sarah's grief at barrenness; her advice that Abraham take Hagar; Hagar's pride and flight, rejecting just punishment (2265b ff.); her exile-sorrow:

> "Nu sceal tearighleor
> on westenne witodes bidan,
> hwonne of heortan hunger laðte wulf
> sawle and sorge somed abregde."
>
> (2276b–79)

She receives the angel's promise and accepts her place.

2304–23. God's contract with Abraham—in return for Abraham's love and loyalty, a mighty line through Sarah; Abraham's request of greatness for Ishmael's line; Sarah's disbelief (2382 ff.). Emphasis throughout is on God's gifts to his own, summarized in the authorial recapitulations, 2377b ff.

VII. The Destruction of Sodom

2399–2599. God's wrath at Sodomites "forþon wælogona sint" (2411b; cf. 2505b). Their sin is betrayal of the chieftain:

> ... hie firendæda   to frece wurdon,
> synna þriste,   so ofergeaton,
> drihtnes domas,   and hwa him dugeða forgeaf,
> blæd on burgum.
>
> (2582–85a)

Cf. 2421 ff. Lot, in contrast, is a loyal servant ("þeow," 2431b) who remembers *ræd* (2462b, 2465b, etc.) and *riht* (2434a, 2478b, etc.) and who fears God's power (2591 ff.). Lot's flight to Zoar and the destruction of the city, presented in images at times recalling the Flood—e.g.,

>   Lagustreamas wreah,
> þrym mid þystro   þisses lifes,
> sæs and sidland.
>
> (2451b–53a)

2600–2620. Lot's drunkenness, his progeny by daughters. (Lacuna at 2599+ makes poetic purpose uncertain.)

VIII. Abraham and Abimelech

2621–2759. Abimelech unwittingly takes Abraham's wife, incurs God's wrath; his race is barren until Abraham pleads for him. Emphasis throughout on God's powerful befriending of Abraham when he is not among human friends (2626–27).

IX. Abraham and Isaac

2760–71. Conception of Isaac, a fulfillment of God's "wordbeot" (2762b); Abraham blesses him, as God bids.

2772–2806. Youth of Isaac, exile of Hagar and Ishmael.

2807–45. Abimelech gives kingdom to Abraham. (Section oddly placed in MS; might more smoothly follow 2627.) Abimelech's request for an exchange of pledges directly echoes God's exchange of pledges at 2306 ff., and the ironic connection shows God's power in contrast to a mortal king's. The irony becomes explicit: whereas Abimelech's gifts come to nothing (2834–37a, where the Hebrews are "feasceaft mid fremdum"), God's gift of a new kingdom (2837b–39) has value.

2846–end. The sacrifice of Isaac, in which Abraham proves his love and dread of God (2862) and God proves worthy of trust. Verbal emphasis is on the fire and sword ("ad," "bælfyr," "sweordes ecge," "forbærnan," all in just four lines, 2856–59; cf. 2888 ff.), and on heights and depths ("steape dune," 2854b, "hrincg þæs hean landes," 2855a, "deop wæter," 2876, "hea rune," 2878b, etc.).

When the poem has been divided into rhetorical units, as above, the poet's principles of selection become clear. Section I (God and Lucifer) presents the secure-kingdom-exile contrast and identifies disloyalty with chieftain-betrayal and kin-betrayal. Section II (Adam and Eve) presents another case of exile from a secure kingdom, this time for chieftain-betrayal. Section III (Cain and Abel) presents Cain's exile for kinsman-betrayal and contrasts the sorrows of the exiled line with the joys of the loyal (1104–27). Section IV (The Flood) contrasts the joys of those loyal to their chieftain (Noah, the dove, Noah's loyal sons) with the sorrows or death (=darkness, =metaphoric exile) of, first, those who marry daughters of Cain; second, the raven; third, the disloyal Ham. The curse of Ham (1695) echoes God's curse of Eve and looks forward to the focus on Hagar's station as "þeow." In section V (Babel), men loving to their kinsmen but proud toward God are exiled from their paradiselike kingdom (1657b, etc.). Section VI (Abraham) contrasts the joys and physical security of the loyal with the sorrow and vulnerability of the disloyal. In the rhetorical unit 1960–2095, the rhythmically encoded emphasis on women (1970a, 1972a, 2009b, 2010a, 2033a, 2086b, etc.) supports the focal idea that God can protect the weak (cf. Abraham's small force). The Elamites are disloyal to kinsmen and friends; they contrast with Abraham, who is loyal to Lot, and contrast with Abraham's loyal friends (2025a, etc.). The section fittingly closes with God's contract with Abraham, gift-giving in return for thanely obedience and love. Section VII (The Destruction of Sodom) contrasts the salvation of Lot for loyalty to God with the destruction of those disloyal to God (2582 ff.). Verbal echoes link the destructive fire with Noah's Flood (e.g., 2451b ff.), Zoar with Noah's Ark. Noah goes "under bord" 1369b (other covering images occur at 1357a, 1360b, 1377b, etc.), and Lot goes "under burhlocan," 2539b (cf. 2489a), a word which at the same time recalls the rhythmically encoded *locking* of the Ark (1391b, 1409b, 1433, etc.). Involved in Lot's loyalty to God is his virtuous behavior to God's "friends," the celestial messengers whom the Sodomites mistreat. (Cf. the disloyal friendliness of Noah's generation to God's enemies.) Section VIII (Abraham and Abimelech) shows in another way God's value as protector of his friends and giver (or withholder) of treasures (lineage is denied to Abimelech). God's power, compared to any earthly king's, is shown by the fact that human kings dare not mistreat God's friends (section VII), but can be enriched by them. The relevance of section IX (Abraham and Isaac) is self-evident. Note that Abraham, befriended by God, can help Abimelech, but Abimelech can give no lasting good to Abraham (another evidence of God's praiseworthy power). As for the rest, Isaac's story shows God's trustworthiness to those loyal to him and shows the law love-thy-kinsman to be secondary to the law love-thy (heavenly)-king.

At this point, no detailed textual analysis should be necessary to demonstrate that the poem has rhetorical design. It will be sufficient to show that certain concepts and images are rhythmically encoded in the poem as a whole. All of these concepts and images have traditional exegetical meaning, but one need not know patristic exegesis to understand them. In the opening episode of the poem, the contrast between heaven and hell—God's kingdom and the place of exile—is underscored by an insistent contrast between light and dark. Thus, later images of light and dark inevitably carry an eschatological burden, patristic exegesis or no. Anything that is emphatically presented in the poem as *light,* like heaven, is typic of heaven or else, as in the case of Cain's daughters or the plains of Sodom, is a false paradise (or false treasure) which will ultimately go dark. Images of greenness, silver, and gold, as well as women's "shining" beauty, elaborate the pattern of light imagery (all aspects of meadhall-joy, or Teutonic Aasgaard as opposed to Utgaard). Dark earth, dark flames, dark water, dark sky, etc., elaborate the darkness-exile pattern. Another pattern, the poem's recurrent image of "high hills," sometimes suggesting heaven, sometimes figuring as a false hope (like the high hills flooded in Noah's day), further develops the safe-kingdom–exile contrast. Finally, the concepts *ræd* and *unræd* are rhythmically encoded. Needless to say, some of the encoded details are present in the biblical passages which served as the poet's source, others are not.

The following incomplete list of word, image, or concept repetitions will be sufficient to show the presence of the encoding. (Numerous additional patterns could be pointed out—for instance, *frofre,* words like *ofostlice* showing quick obedience, and the phrase "lufum and lissum.")

Light, spaciousness, greenness.—Lines 10–12a, 14a, 28a, 31a, 86b–89a, 95a, 100a, 104b, 114b, 118b, 119b, 122b, 123a, 124b, 127b, 128a, 129b, 131a, 134b, 137a, 144a, 156a, 167b, 175a, 188a, 197a, 198b–200a, 206–12a, 220a, 223, 224b–27a, 230a, 234b, 853a, 857b, 890a, 907b, 926a, 956b, 957, 1017b, 1018a, 1136b, 1137a, 1166, 1243a, 1252, 1260, 1293,

1331b, 1371b, 1392–93, 1410a, 1416a, 1428b, 1429b, 1445a, 1454a, 1455a, 1456a, 1458b, 1465b, 1470, 1474a, 1480a, 1502a, 1517a, 1560, 1661b, 1599b, 1651b, 1655b, 1657b, 1658a, 1659a, 1717b, 1728a, 1751a, 1752a, 1787b, 1789a, 1792a, 1804, 1807a, 1822a, 1827a, 1828a, 1848a, 1850a, 1852b, 1855a, 1889, 1921b, 1923, 1933b, 2191–94, 2377a, 2408b, 2423a, 2450a, 2551a, 2731a, 2875b. (This list does not include words inherently associated with light or space, such as *sinc, engla, heofon,* unless modifiers involving light or space are present.)

Darkness, sorrows-of-exile.—Lines 37a, 42a, 44a, 67b–76, 85, 86a, 90–91, 103b, 105, 108b–10a, 117–19a, 125a, 127b, 128a, 133b, 134a, 137a, 139a, 140a, 144a, 155b, 212b–15a, 859, 860a, 874, 876b, 904b, 906–910a, 919–921, 927–28a, 943b–45a, 961b, 962, 964, 1015–18a, 1020b–21, 1023–26, 1032–33a, 1047b–53a, 1294a, 1300b–1301a, 1325b–26a, 1355a, 1375a, 1379a, 1414a, 1430a, 1431b–35, 1441b–42a, 1448a, 1449b, 1461a, 1462a, 1481a, 1523b, 1526, 1595a, 1673b, 1925b, 1926b, 1983b, 2060b, 2064a, 2082a, 2267b–68a, 2277–79, 2281a, 2289–92, 2417–18, 2450b–53a, 2479–82a, 2507b, 2822–23, 2858b, 2874a, 2875a. (This list does not include things inherently dark, such as the raven, unless the darkness is specified.)

Heights, depths.—Lines 21a, 40a, 50a, 70b, 97a, 98a, 99b, 146b, 1387b, 1397b–98a, 1401b, 1419b, 1421b–22a, 1439a, 1451a, 1459b, 1821b, 2214a, 2404a, 2405–6, 2420a, 2519a, 2520a, 2522–26a, 2571b, 2579b–80, 2840b–41a, 2854b–55a, 2878b. (This list excludes direct references to the heavens—but see 21a—and excludes the pattern of images involving coveredness [e.g., of Adam: 868b, etc.; of Noah: 1357a, 1360b, 1369b, etc.; of Cain: 1585b–86a, etc.]; and the list ignores seemingly unavoidable and automatic uses of *deop.*)

Ræd and unræd.—Lines 9a, 21b, 24a, 30a, 44b, 51b, 169a, 982b, 1195b, 1266a, 1287a, 1292a, 1319b, 1346b–47a, 1446b, 1498a, 1625a, 1671b–74a, 1682b, 1732a, 1780a, 1795b–97, 1913b, 1937a, 1956–59, 2119, 2182a, 2247, 2434a, 2462b, 2478, 2505b, 2583, 2598, 2807–10, 2862a, 2893b–94, 2901a. (This list could be expanded indefinitely as *ræd* shades off into the connotative deomains of *soð, swiðfeorm,* etc.)

Examination of these lists will show that repetitions tend to come in clusters, rhetorically linking certain episodes with others, so that, for instance, the expulsion of the disloyal angels is verbally linked with the exiles of Adam, Cain, Noah's generation, etc. The rhythmic encoding, in other words, suggests allegorical intent on the part of the poet. At times this intent is explicit, as in the poet's *interpretatio* on the tree in Eden (987 ff.); at other times the possibility of allegory is a matter for individual interpretation, as at 2887b–88a, "Wudu bær sunu,/fæder fyr and sweord," where Christ's carrying of the cross and the Father's destruction of the world may or may not be suggested. But whatever one's judgment of particular details, an allegorical reading of events in the poem is stylistically urged by thematic *repetitio* in the poem itself; the allegory is not brought over by accident from the source.

Genesis B

An obvious test of this reading of *Genesis A* is *Genesis B*, a poem we know to have been separately composed and inserted in *Genesis A*.[12]

Genesis B has little in common with *Genesis A*. In place of the earlier poem's subtle development of metaphoric ideas (heaven as secure kingdom, hell as "paths of exile"), *Genesis B* has an insistent hellfire literalness which excludes any such metaphor. Whereas *Genesis A* consistently makes use of words like *ræd,* which apply equally well to order in earthly courts and to the just rule of the cosmos, *Genesis B* uses locutions such as "halige word" (245; cf. 428b, 430a, 537a, etc.), which enforce a literal view of the biblical events. (It may be observed, by the way, that whereas *ræd* is always used straight in *Genesis A,* the more elaborately dramatized *Genesis B* at times uses *ræd,* and also *riht,* etc., within limited-point-of-view statements—i.e., *ræd* as it seems to Lucifer or Eve.)

The sorrow motif in *Genesis A* has its complement in *Genesis B,* but here torment, punishment, and slavery to devils (*not* exile) are the ideas rhetorically emphasized. Such words as *wræclast* never appear. Hell is *helle* in *Genesis B* (e.g., 303a), a distinct "oþer land" (332b) which Lucifer must care for (345–49) and where he is a prisoner in shackles (434a, 762a, 765, etc.). The emphasis in the poet's treatment of the Fall is not on Adam and Eve's betrayal of their chieftain and consequent exile into wilderness; it is on the guile (445b–46, 703, 711, etc.) and fiendish "cræft" (453, 492b, etc.) of Satan, who tricks the couple into falling not despite God's command but in obedience to it, as they fancy. Satan makes Eve believe God has commanded her to eat the poison fruit, and Eve convinces Adam because, tricked by a false vision of beauty, she "wende þæt heo hyldo heofon cyninges/worhte" (712–13a). Satan, when not viewed as a prisoner in a dungeon, is seen as an enemy king (407, 409 ff., 450, 487a, etc.) out to steal God's "gingran" (458b) to make them his slaves (407, 450, etc.). Numerous other details exclude the *A*-poet's metaphoric treatment of heaven and hell. One of the most striking is the transmogrification of the fallen angels from creatures of light and beauty to creatures deformed and dark (308–9; cf. 338–39).

As in *Genesis A,* light and darkness are an important contrast in *Genesis B,* but the contrast serves a new function. Light is associated simply with good, darkness with evil; the more specific *Genesis A* contrast (joys of the meadhall, sorrows of exile) is entirely absent. Before his fall, Lucifer is as bright as the stars (256), "leoht and scene,/hwit and heowbeorht" (265b–66a). Eve, too, is identified with light (821b–22a). The good and evil trees in the garden contrast in that one is light, one dark (467–76, 477–89a). Satan's whole temptation is a false offer of light and beauty (502, 564–65, 603–9, 611–22, 666–77, 700–701, 704, 772); and the fallen couple's realization of their mistake comes when Eve's illusory vision fades and they know that the darkness of death and hell is now their lot (685a, 731–40a, 745–55, 761–65a, 765b–77a, 792b–95a, 799b–815).

The whole rhetorical method of *Genesis B* is radically different from that of *Genesis A.* In the earlier poem meaning is implied by structural parallels underscored by the rhythmic encoding of thematically important images, words, and concepts. In the later poem the poet's main ideas are hammered home by openly and literally repetitive blocks of rant concerning the joy of heaven and the importance of keeping God's commandments because of the bitterness of hell. Because the *B*-poet's controlling ideas are clear and simple (salvation, obedience, damnation), and because he depends much more heavily than did the *A*-poet on long set speeches, the structure of *Genesis B* needs no detailed analysis. Three rhetorical units can stand for the whole. In lines 304–54, the poet narrates Satan's disobedience, tells of the dreadfulness of hell, and contrasts the bliss of heaven. In lines 355–440, Satan himself talks of the dreadfulness of hell, contrasts hell's torment with the bliss of heaven and the bliss of Eden, and resolves in spite to make Adam disobedient to God's command. In lines 460–90, the poet contrasts the two trees in Eden, one of which leads to death, darkness, fire, etc., and urges the value of obedience. The poet misses no opportunity to recapitulate his grim story (e.g., 762b ff.) or tell again of the dreadfulness of Hell (as in Adam's lament, 791 ff., which restates Satan's lament 355 ff., and the poet's earlier description of hell, 330 ff.).

Both poets, of course, Teutonicize *Genesis.* In *B,* the thane of Satan who goes to Eden is repaying his lord's gift-giving, and hell is, among other things, a substitute for the "timbered building" Satan meant to set up in heaven (276). The difference is that in *Genesis A* the Teutonicizing goes beyond surface detail to *schemata.* That difference, needless to say, implies another. The *A*-poet concerns himself with relationships between native Teutonic values and Christian doctrine. The *B*-poet's concern is with heightening the biblical drama and frightening the unfaithful with pictures of hell. *A,* but not *B,* has rhetorical sophistication like that which has been noticed in Caedmon's *Hymn.*

Daniel

The same general sort of rhythmic encoding can be found in *Daniel.* Like *Genesis A,* the Caedmonic *Daniel* probably contains at least one major interpolation, the prayer at lines 279–361, which has been preserved separately in the Exeter Book (the "Azarias") and which seems oddly placed within *Daniel.* Gollancz suggested that the hymn should go after line 231, not after 278 where it appears, and he believed that the interpolater went on too long, since lines 336–56a repeat material already paraphrased in 232 ff. On Gollancz' theory Professor Krapp comments: "This may be the right explanation of the presence of the Prayer in *Daniel,* but it should be pointed out that even if the Prayer had been interpolated, or inserted by the poet himself, after 1.231, it would still have been awkward to have this somewhat long irrelevant lyric thrust in just at a moment of high suspense in the action."[13] Krapp is suggesting—if I understand his cryptic remark—that the poet may have finished out his story to line 278 and may then have doubled back on the story to elaborate it with the prayer (and also the Song of Praise by the three in the furnace) *after* "high suspense in the action" was no longer a concern. Krapp's suggestion might be convincing except for *þa* in line 279, which implies profluent narration.

But whatever one's stand on the possibly interpolated lines, the Caedmonic *Daniel* is rhetorically well made, and if the questionable lines are an interpolation, as I think they are, they were inserted by someone who understood the main themes of the poem he was expanding. (In two respects, as we will see, the possibly interpolated lines do not seem to fit; but the evidence is far from conclusive.)

The first of the controlling ideas in *Daniel* is stock in Old English biblical verse translation: obedience to God wins characteristically Teutonic tribal wealth and strength: "goldhord" and "cyningdom" (2b, 3a). The poem's second controlling idea is also stock but is developed in an original fashion: the idea is that pride (rising above one's station) is a betrayal of God's rule and brings on punishment. For development of this idea, the poet takes details from the Nebuchadnezzar-Belshazzar story and introduces them throughout his poem to establish an allegorical relationship between events. By introducing metaphorical and nonscriptural allusions to drunkenness throughout the poem, the poet makes Belshazzar's drunkenness representative of all *unræd* grounded on foolish pride. By extending Nebuchadnezzar's worship of idols (devil worship) through allusion to all proud thought as "devilish" and by identifying Nebuchadnezzar's worship of a golden figure with any misuse of worldly things (*eorðan dreamas*) the poet symbolically generalizes Nebuchadnezzar's mistake. Against these symbolic treatments of *unræd*, and against the literal treatments of *unræd* in Nebuchadnezzar's madness and Belshazzar's drunkenness, the poet plays his main theme, right reason—a theme he presents by tour de force rhythmic encoding, and a theme either he or some later poet further developed in the Prayer of Azarias and the *Hymnum trium puerorum*.

The first controlling idea—that obedience brings wealth and power —is explicit in the poem's opening lines (1–16), in Nebuchadnezzar's success when he is sent by God to chastize the overweening Jews (39 ff), and again when Nebuchadnezzar wisely accepts God's rule (640–70). Nebuchadnezzar's line is powerful and wealthy (671–74) until the moment of Belshazzar's lapse into "wlenco" (677b) and "oferhyd" (678a); then God transfers wealth and power to the Medes and Persians (680 ff). Pride is frequently treated in *Daniel*, as in other Caedmonic poetry, as an exaggerated sense of one's own puissance (cf. 598 ff), reflected in overconfident war boasts. (Forms of *gylp* occur at lines 598, 612, 635, 694, 711, 712, 715, 754.) But early in the poem pride is also presented as a kind of drunkenness. The overconfident Jews of the first episode are metaphorically "winþege" (17b) and "druncne" (18b). When Nebuchadnezzar awakens, clear-headed, from his *somnium coeleste,* he is described (literally) as "ær wingal" (116b). Belshazzar's mistake, too, comes in part from literal drunkenness (see, e.g., 695a, 702a, 752a).

Drunk or sober, the man too proud to serve God is a servant of the devil. The proud Jews of the first episode do "drunken devil-deeds" (18a), choose "deofles cræft" (32b); in doing so—in overvaluing golden figures by supposing them inspirited—they succumb to a specific kind of pride, "anmedlan in æht" (747). They forget the *soð* implied in the contrast of temple treasures and Belshazzar's treasures (681 ff.), the *soð* expounded in the poem's last surviving lines, that God is the ruler of treasures and possessions (760–62), the ruler even of devils (764). What right reason grasps—and what Nebuchadnezzar learns in his first prophetic nightmare—is that the pleasures of this world (*eor an dreamas*) pass away (114–15), so that only God can be trusted. The contrast, established at the start of the poem, is between *rædas* and *eorðan dreamas* (30).

The thematic centrality of the idea "right reason" in the Caedmonic *Daniel* can be suggested by a list of occurrences of words like *wisdom, snytro, lare, rædas, domes,* etc., that is, words involving the connotational domain of wisdom. How thickly such words are encoded in the poem can be seen in passages like this one:

> Oft he þam leodum   to *lare* sende,
> heofonrices weard,   halige gastas,
> þa þam werude   *wisdom* budon.
> Hie þære *snytro*   soð *gelyfdon*
> lytle hwile,   oðþæt hie langung beswac
> eorðan dreamas   eces *rædas,*
> þæt hie æt siðestan   sylfe forleton
> drihtnes *domas,*   curon deofles *cræfte.*
>
> (25–32: my italics)

The following list of occurrences of such words is meant to be suggestive, not complete: Lines 25, 27, 28, 30, 32, 81b, 83b, 84a, 94a, 96b, 98a, 113b, 132b, 135b, 137a, 138b, 142b, 143b, 144a, 146a, 149b, 150a, 151a, 155a, 160a, 161, 164b, 176a, 177a, 182b, 184b, 186a, 203, 205b, 217b, 268, 332, 416b, 417a, 420a, 426a, 439a, 444a, 445a, 446a, 450b, 459b, 467, 477, 485, 486b, 533b, 535, 536, 543, 546b, 547a, 549, 565a, 571, 585, 594, 614, 623, 627a, 629b, 630b, 634a, 639, 646, 651, 657b, 660b, 661a, 666a, 685b, 702b, 731b, 733, 736a, 737b, 740, 741a, 742b, 744a, 758a.

Examination of this list shows that in the possibly interpolated Prayer of Azarias, as well as in the *Hymnum trium puerorum* (362–408), which rhetorically balances the prayer and may also be an interpolation (though Gollancz did not suspect it to be one), there are virtually no occurrences of words rhythmically encoded in support of the right reason theme. Neither do these passages include allusions to drunkenness or to devil worship, and the hymn of the three in the furnace does not even treat worldly treasures. In the hymn God's gifts to man are not treasure and tribal power but natural blessings, earth's weather and the like. But this does not prove the passages interpolated.

The prayer comes in three rhetorical units:

1. a. God's power and majesty as protector (283–85).
   b. God's lawfulness and truth (286–88).

c. God's right will about worldly wealth, property of the obedient (289–90).

2. The three victims' plea for help though help is not fully deserved (291–99b); a recognition of why the race is scattered and the people enslaved (300–308).

3. A plea that God remember his promise to Abraham, Isaac, and Jacob, and show the Chaldeans his might (309–37).

For all its lack of the elsewhere rhythmically encoded details, the passage shows the *ræd* of Azarias as surely as the passage on Nebuchadnezzar's madness shows his *unræd*. It shows his recognition that the Jews have been guilty of pride and ends with an appeal that the old contract be fulfilled by "soðfæst Metod" (337). The angel of God comes with mercy and "migtasped" (334) and turns the fire against the enemy, a proof of God's protective might. The hymn of the three in the furnace is equally relevant to the poem as a whole: It praises God not for those pleasures of earth delightful to the sinfully concupiscent—gold and the like (these are not mentioned)—but for life and joy in life, for which all Nature is grateful, and it emphasizes the point that the gift is given to the obedient ("lean sellende / eallum eadmodum"—395b–96a). Thus the possibly interpolated passages support the theme of the whole, though they lack the poem's most obvious rhetorical keys.

Whether or not the doubtful passages are authentic, the greater part of *Daniel* works like *Genesis A:* its separate episodes are linked by verbal repetition or other forms of cross-reference which give allegorical resonance to the whole.

Now let us compare the quasi-Caedmonic, quasi-Cynewulfian *Christ and Satan*.

Christ and Satan

Christ and Satan begins in the premises we find behind all Caedmonic poetry and which I have pointed out in *Genesis A* and *Daniel:* God is viewed as a Teutonic king—a protector and treasure-giver— and Satan is viewed as an exile, here an exiled usurper who continues to plot against the king but is finally overwhelmed. As in *Genesis A* and *Daniel,* the poet's method is allegorical; but here the allegorical method is more transparent than that in earlier Caedmonic verse. In the earlier poetry (as, also, in poems like Cynewulf's *Elene*) separate episodes within a narrative are significantly linked by verbal repetition or other echoing devices, with the result that allegory emerges from the line of episodes, not from episodes taken singly: in *Christ and Satan*, there is of course no true narrative, hence no *linear* allegory. The deeper meaning of events recounted is extracted by authorial commentary: Satan is an example of what man ought not to be and Christ is an example of the ideal toward which man should strive. Intrusive commentary occurs, for instance, at lines 193–223, beginning:

> Forþan sceal gehycgan   hæleða æghwylc
> þæt he ne abælige   bearn waldendes.
> Læte him to bysne   hu þa blacan feond
> for oferhygdum   ealle forwurdon.
> Neoman us to wynne   weoroda drihten,
> uppe ecne gefean,   engla wandend . . .
>
> (193–96)

The poet pauses frequently for commentary on Satan and Christ as wrong and right models, for instance at lines 279–314, 549–56, 593b–96, and 643–58. In theme, the poem is related to *Genesis A* and *Daniel*— the supreme power of God and the vulnerability of those who, like Satan, would raise themselves above him. The theme is explicit at various points, e.g., 32–33, 193–201, 282–300, 348–52, 582–84, 642–69. Structurally, the poem is developed in three sections, the first (1–365) dealing mainly with Satan's unsuccessful attempt at usurpation and intepreted by the poet as archtypical of pride; the second (366–664) dealing with Christ's victories in the harrowing of hell, the Resurrection, the Ascension, and the Last Judgment, interpreted by the poet as proof of divine power; and the final section dealing with Christ's face-to-face confrontation with Satan during the temptation in the wilderness, implicitly a model of steadfastness for man.

Obviously the poem is not an example of Caedmonic *translatio* (but then, neither is Caedmon's *Hymn*), and though it looks forward, or else dim-wittedly backward, to the more complex Cynewulfian meditations—*Christ, Guthlac,* and the like—it is not respectably Cynewulfian either. *Christ and Satan,* whether it was actually written early or late, is stylistically transitional. It is vaguely Cynewulfian in structure, the poet having abandoned chronology for a thematic principle of progression; but it is solidly Caedmonic in its premises— that God and Satan are opposing treasure-givers, one true, one false (cf. *brytan,* 23, 123, etc.), and that hell is a place of exile (cf. 120, 187, 257, etc.).

These premises are the root of Caedmonic style. It may be that they originated when an extraordinary cowherd turned Teutonic concepts of the protector, fighter, hall-builder to a new purpose: *heofonrices weard; meotodes meahte; heofon to hrofe; moncynnes weard; frea ælmihtig* (Caedmon's *Hymn,* 1b, 2a, 6a, 7b, 9b). But in any event, the metaphoric premises that God is a chieftain, heaven a secure kingdom, hell a place of exile—these are the gift of the Caedmonic school to later religious poetry in Old English. The characteristic development of these premises in Caedmonic verse is an application of exegetical principles of *translatio,* wherein the source is curtailed, amplified, interpreted, and so forth for focus on particular themes, and wherein key words, images, and concepts are rhythmically encoded into the poetic texture for linear allegory.[14] Later religious poetry in Old English generally maintains the Caedmonic premises but shifts to more complex forms of development (from biblical subject matter to pagan, as in *Beowulf;* from relatively simple linear allegory to more complicated allegory, as in *Beowulf* and *Elene*) and from narrative to lyrical meditation, as in *Christ and Satan* or *Guthlac.*

3

From the Riddle to
the Christian Elegy

Caedmonic poetry of the *Genesis A* type offers one stylistic option
for the construction of allegory—the linear method. Another method
has its logical beginning in the riddle, evolves to a technique of image
and interpretation (the *Physiologus* and *Phoenix*), then to a technique
we may call symbolic. This last is the technique of the Christian
elegies, in which an image is presented in such a way that it is at
once literal and iconographic. As later chapters will show, in *Beowulf*
and in the most complex of the Cynewulfian poems the linear and
nonlinear styles of allegory are brought together. Both styles are of
course present in scripture as the exegetes read it, and it goes without
saying that poets constructed their allegories in imitation of the
scriptural method.[1] But the poets' debt to exegetes need not delay us.
What is of interest at the moment is, first, the particular devices with
which Anglo-Saxon poets built their allegories and, second, the coherence of their tradition with respect to poetic allegory. As we will
see, not only for general techniques but sometimes even for specific
figurae, the *Beowulf*-poet and Cynewulf turn to earlier English poets.

Linear allegory like that in *Genesis A* is set up, we have observed, by
rhythmic encoding: key words, images, or concepts are repeated to
establish connections between segments of the poem—commonly,
connections between episodes of a narrative. Obviously the poet
presenting a narrative of only one scene or presenting a poem which
focuses on a character or image cannot set up allegory in the cumula-

tive way, through rhythmic encoding of the kind in *Genesis A*. In the one-scene or one-image poem, allegory must come through the poet's treatment of individual details which together make up the scene or image. By his handling of language he must imply more than he says, making the listener feel unsatisfied with a literal understanding of the poem. Besides the technique of allusion (a matter I leave to others, since it has been much discussed of late), the poet has only two choices: (1) he may emphasize some single detail or group of details, making that detail or group stand out in the foreground of the poem curiously overshadowing surrounding details not less important logically (i.e., he may use *kosmoi*), and (2) he may use language which calls up a context of experience foreign to the one literally represented (i.e., he may depend on syntactic implication). In either case, the result is a kind of "vertical" allegory in which poetic implication depends on texture, not structural echo.

Whether the Old English riddle was inspired by Latin models or existed as an Anglo-Saxon genre before the entrance of Christianity,[2] the riddles provide a logical starting point for an examination of vertical allegory in Old English poetry. The primary technique of the riddles is a deliberate obfuscation of verbal context for one purpose or another—that is, in order that the listener may be misled, to his own humiliation (as in the obscene riddles), in order that he may be thrown off the track (in riddles intended as puzzles), in order that he may be forced to conflicting solutions and delight in the riddler's dexterity, or, finally, in order that he may be stirred to religious awe, as in the storm riddles. What counts, for our study, is the technique common to all these forms, the obfuscation of verbal context which produces thick—or "ambiguous," or "rich"—texture.

Consider the "obscene" onion riddle:

> Ic eom wunderlicu wiht, wifum on hyhte,
> neahbuendum nyt; nængum sceþþe
> burgsittendra, nymþe þonan anum.
> Staþol min is steapheah, stonde ic on bedde,
> neoþan ruh nathwær. Neþeð hwilum
> ful cyrtenu ceorles dohtor,
> modwlonc meowle, þæt heo on mec gripeð,
> raeseð mec on reodne, reafað min heafod,
> fegeð mec fæsten. Feleþ sona
> mines gemotes, seo þe mec nearwað,
> wif wundenlocc. Waet bið þæt eage.[3]

The opening statement here suggests, by the phrases "a delight to women" and "useful to neighbors," some household object; but the listener's decision is tentative, since *wiht* may be a creature, not a thing, and *hyhte,* though it can mean, simply, "joy," has a strong sense of *"expected* joy" or "hope." The second statement abruptly shifts from the household context to imply something somehow military, the context of words like *sceppe* and *bonan;* but again the decision is tentative, since *burgsittendra* fits both contexts—"villagers" versus "occupants of the stronghold." In the third statement (4–5a), the solution to the riddle suddenly seems clear: though the phrase "Staþol min is steapheah" has possible military associations, in connection with "bed" and "I am shaggy below," and in connection, too, with the earlier phrases "delight to women" (now the overtone-meaning of *hyhte* comes ludicrously clear) and "useful to neighbors," the obscene context leaps to mind. The remainder of the poem ingeniously elaborates this "false" verbal context in terms also applicable to the "true," innocent context, a girl's pulling of an onion.

The same technique devoted to a rather different end partly accounts for the richness and power of the storm riddles. These, of course, are riddles only in an extended sense. Like Blake's "Tyger, Tyger," they close with rhetorical questions which, though answerable, cannot adequately be answered except by awe. The chief interest lies in the descriptions not because they are puzzling but because they are metaphorically complex. Throughout Riddle #1 it is clear that the speaker is a destructive storm on land, possibly the storm of Noah's time. (Professor Baum confidently asserts that lines 12–14 "refer to the Biblical Flood."[4] This seems to me wrong, since there is a better explanation of 13b.) But the poem has overtone solutions built into it: the storm is like a preying beast, like a savage exile, and like something or someone out of hell.

>Hwylc is hæleþa þæs horsc   ond þæs hygecræftig
>þaet þaet mæge asecgan,   hwa mec on sið wræce,
>þonne ic astige strong,   stundum reþe,
>þrymful þunie,   þragum wræce
>fare geond foldan,   folcsalo bærne,
>ræced reafige?   Recas stigað,
>haswe ofer hrofum.   Hlin bið on eorþan,
>wælcwealm wera,   þonne ic wudu hrere,
>bearwas bledhwate,   beamas fylle,
>holme gehrefed,   heahum meahtum
>wrecen on waþe,   wide sended;

heabbe me on hrycge   þæt ær hadas wreah
foldbuendra,   flæsc ond gæstas,
somod on sunde.   Saga hwa mec þecce,
oþþe hu ic hatte,   þe þa hlæst bere.[5]

The context set up in the opening line is one of war or, perhaps, hunting. The listener is addressed as "hæleþa"—compare the effect of possible alternatives like "ylda bearn"—and he is exhorted to be *horsc* and *hygecræftig*, words which place ready-wittedness and skillfulness-of-mind in the context of battle. The word *sið*, though it may refer to any journey, is commonly associated with war expeditions, and *wræce* (2), though it can mean simply "drive out," usually has the sense "punish," "drive into exile," etc. The word *astige* is as applicable to warriors as to winds and thunderheads; *stundum* has, besides the common sense (at certain seasons or times), the military and hunting sense (at certain signals—cf. *Beowulf*, 2851); *reþe* has a connotative domain extending from "justly wrathful" to "savage" (of men or beasts) and has common associations with fierce punishing. Throughout the remainder of the poem the poet continues to select words and images which suggest a warlike context, metaphorically equating the storm and battle. Along with these he chooses words and images suggesting the miseries of exile (*wraece*, 4b, *wrecen on waþe, wide sended*, 11), and words which suggest possible identification of the speaker in the poem with some savage beast of prey (*hrycge*, 12a, which can mean a beast's hump; *waþe*, 11a, in the sense "hunting"; and cf. the image of shaking trees, 8b–9). These blurred associations give force to the closing question, "Saga hwa mec þecce, / oþþe hu ic hatte, þe þa hlæst bere." The destroyer of things which protect and cover men (*folcsalo*, 5b, etc.) is, though an exile, somehow unthinkably roofed or covered itself (*þecce*, 14b); in other words, imitating the technique of the mystic, the poet praises God partly by making him the resolver of contradiction. If we add to our reading of the poem the common Caedmonic extension of the idea of exile, then the idea of punishment or hell-torment in *wræce* (4), the images of fiery destruction in lines 5b–7a, the suggestion of murderous hunting, involving the death of both "flæsc" and "gæstas" (13b), and, finally, the secondary sense of *hlæst* (15b), in which the word refers not simply to the houses borne on the storm's back but also to some spiritual burden of misery—all these combine to suggest identification of the storm and demonic powers. The difficulty in the question "Saga . . . hu ic hatte," then, is that nothing man knows provides an emotionally satisfying answer—

the poet has called up, through the storm, the whole idea of evil—
and the incredible might of God rests, here as in the Caedmonic
Daniel, in his kingship even over hell.

It should be observed that allegory—or language enrichment—of
this kind is far more subtle than linear allegory and tends to leave
interpretation open. Whereas rhythmic encoding can be pointed out
as a fact of the poem in which it appears, so that the presence of the
resulting allegory is indisputable, allegory developed through syntactic
implication—and also, we may add, allegory developed through
kosmoi, for instance the figures of the Seafarer and Wanderer—is likely
to be obvious to some readers, invisible to others. The prejudiced
critic may argue that the reader who does not (or does) see the allegory
is an insensitive clod, but such argument misses the heart of the matter:
an unsophisticated poet struggling for words to express his feeling
about storms might unconsciously produce a poem drawing on contexts of war, hunting, and demonic exile—the same poem an allegorist
might produce on purpose. The poet's intent is, if not unknowable,
unprovable. The only argument the critic can finally offer for his
allegorical reading of the poem is that many poems work in the same
way, and work with perfect consistency, while other poems—the
critic's control—do not. The likelihood that the Caedmonic extension
of the idea of exile (hell = exile) is meant to be caught in Riddle #1
comes mainly from the fact that the same extension appears in various
Caedmonic poems, in *Beowulf,* and in several Cynewulfian poems, and
in those cases is provable, nonsubjective. But analogy and probability
do not constitute proof. The chief aesthetic virtue of the kind of allegory being examined in this chapter is that within short poems it is
always more or less nebulous, impossible to strip of all ambiguity. The
Seafarer debate, however absurd to men of sense, can never be fully
resolved.

Metaphoric enrichment through context blurring is also present in
the second of the storm riddles (that is, the second and third Exeter
riddles which actually comprise, most scholars now agree, one riddle
in four parts and a conclusion).[6]

> Hwilum ic gewite,   swa ne wenaþ men,
> under yþa geþræc   eorþan secan,
> garescges grund.   Gifen biþ gewreged,
> fam gewealcen;
> hwælmere hlimmeð,   hlude grimmeð,
> streamas staþu beatað,   stundum weorpaþ
> on stealc hleoþa   stane ond sonde,

ware ond wæge, þonne ic winnende,
holmmægne biþeaht, hrusan styrge,
side sægrundas. Sundhelme ne mæg   10
losian ær mec læte se þe min latteow bið
on siþa gehwam. Saga, þoncol mon,
hwa mec bregde of brimes fæþmum,
þonne streamas eft stille weorþað
yþa geþwaere, þe mec ær wrugon.
   Hwilum mec min frea fæste genearwað,
sendeð þonne under salwonges
bearm þone bradan, ond on bid wriceð,
þrafað on þystrum þrymma sumne
hæste on enge, þær me heord siteð   20
hruse on hrycge. Nah ic hwyrftweges
of þam aglace, ac ic eþelstol
hæleþa hrere; hornsalu wagiað
wera wicstede, weallas beofiað,
steape ofer stiwitum. Stille þynceð
lyft ofer londe ond lagu swige,
oþþaet ic of enge up aþringe,
efne swa mec wisaþ se mec wræde on
æt frumsceafte furþum legde,
bende ond clomme þæt ic onbugan ne mot   30
of þæs gewealde þe me wegas tæcneð.
   Hwilum ic sceal ufan yþa wregan,
streamas styrgan ond to staþe þywan
flintgrægne flod. Famig winneð
wæg wið wealle, wonn ariseð
dun ofer dype; hyre deorc on last,
eare geblonden, oþer fereð,
þæt hy gemittað mearclonde neah
hea hlincas. þær bið hlud wudu,
brimgiesta breahtm, bidað stille   40
stealc stanhleoþu streamgeminnes,
hopgehnastes, þonne heah geþring
on cleofu crydeþ. þær bið ceole wen
sliþre sæcce, gif hine sae byreð
on þa grimman tid, gæsta fulne,
þæt he scyle rice birofen weorþan,
feore bifohten fæmig ridan
hþa hrycgum. þær bið egsa sum
ældum geywed, þara þe ic hyran sceal
strong on stiðweg. Hwa gestilleð þæt?   50
   Hwilum ic þurhræse, þæt me on bæce rideð
won wægfatu, wide toþringe

lagustreama full,   whilum læte eft
slupan tosomne.   Se bið swega mæst,
breahtma ofer burgum,   ond gebreca hludast,
þonne scearp cymeð   sceo wiþ oþrum,
ecg wið ecge;   earpan gesceafte
fus ofer folcnum   fyre swætað,
blacan lige,   ond gebrecu ferað
deorc ofer dryhtum   gedyne micle,   60
farað feohtende,   feallan lætað
sweart sumsendu   seaw of bosme,
wætan of wombe.   Winnende fareð
atol eoredþreat,   egsa astigeð,
micel modþrea   monna cynne,
brogan on burgum,   þonne blace scotiað
scriþende scin   scearpum wæpnum.
Dol him ne ondrædeð   ða deaðsperu,
swylteð hwæþre,   gif him soð meotud
on geryhtu   þurh regn ufan   70
of gestune læteð   stræle fleogan,
farende flan.   Fea þæt gedygað,
þara þe geræceð   rynegiestes wæpen.
  Ic þæs orleges   or anstelle,
þonne gewite   wolcengehnaste
þurh geþræc þringan   þrimme micle
ofer byrnan bosm.   Biersteð hlude
heah hloðgecrod;   þonne hnige eft
under lyfte helm   londe near,
ond me on hrycg hlade   þæt ic habban sceal,   80
meahtum gemagnad   mines frean.
Swa ic þrymful þeow   þragum winne,
hwilum under eorþan,   hwilum yþa sceal
hean underhnigan,   hwilum holm ufan
streamas styrge,   hwilum stige up,
wolcnfare wrege,   wide fere
swift ond swiþfeorm.   Saga hwæt ic hatte,
oþþa hwa mec rære,   þonne ic restan ne mot,
oþþa hwa mec stæðþe,   þonne ic stille beom.

Like the author of the first storm riddle, the author of the second shows knowledge of ancient cosmology (Plato, Lucretius, Pliny) and medieval theory (Isidore, Bede).[7] His allusions and his selection of details suggest that the answer to his closing question—"Who rouses me?"—must be "Nature"; but explicit references to the speaker's "frea" (16a, my numbering, above) and to the speaker's station as þrymful þeow" (82a) urge a different answer, God, chieftain over Nature.

Throughout the poem, the poet supports his characterization of God as chieftain over natural forces by consistently selecting verbal contexts which anthropomorphize Nature. In the first line, the word *gewite*, alliteratively balanced with *wenaþ* (applied to men) carries overtones of sentience—not simply "go" but "look to go," even shading toward "know," "understand." In line 2, the phrase "yþa geþræc," reinforced by "secan" has clear overtones of "multitude," "crowd,"— the sense of *geþræc* in such locutions as *beorna geþræc*. In such a context, the linguistically frozen metaphor in *garsecges* (3a) has a tendency to thaw, and *grund* hovers between the sense "ground" or "sea-floor" and the sense "realm." The word *gewreged* (3b) can mean simply "stirred up," but in the context of other anthropomorphizing words it takes on the secondary meaning "excited," "stirred to passion." The *hlimmeð, grimmeð, beatað*, and *weorpaþ* all share this contextual doubleness. Thus *staþu* (6a) moves connotatively beyond "firm place," a literal description of the shore, toward *staþol* in the sense of "foundation," "established place," "fort," and the conflict of sea and land becomes metaphoric war. The metaphor is further developed in *winnende* (8b), and in *holmmægne biþeat* (9a). The word *helme* in the compound *Sundhelme* (10b) takes on the sense of anthropomorphic guardianship, implying a guardianship which the poet then explicitly presents as secondary to that of the chieftain (*latteow* [i.e., *lad-teow*], 11b). The phrase *þancol mon* (12b), which begins the close of the rhetorical unit that began with *gewite* and *wenaþ* (1), strikes with ironic force: the riddle question establishes the same opposition— proud man versus Nature—implied in the opening line. The remainder of the riddle question sustains the metaphor of storm as retainer: *fæþmum* (13b) has the sense, beyond "embrace," of "household" or "realm"; the phrase *yþa geþwære* (15a) moves beyond "gentleness" to "concord," "sentient agreement;" and *wrugon* (15b) has the sense, beyond the visual image (covered), of "roofed," or loosely, "domesticated."

In the riddle's second rhetorical unit, lines 16–31 (the storm as earthquake), the anthropomorphizing process continues. Here the storm is confined and tormented like a prisoner (16b) in misery and darkness (22a, 19a) by a powerful lord (16a), and only when that lord allows can the prisoner thrust upward (27–31), escaping his fetters (30a). Again the contrast between man's power and that of the storm is focal: the storm shakes the houses of heroes (22b–23a), and the chieftain's power, far greater even than the storm's, is dramatized (30b–31). The selection of details here suggests a metaphoric identification of the storm and Satan—especially such details as *genearwað* (16b), a word often implying persecution; *þrafað* (19a), often implying rebuke; *aglace* (22a), related to *aglaca,* often used of Satan; *enge* (27a), "prison"; and the image *bende ond clomme* (30a). For the listener who catches this allegorical overtone, the poem becomes a dramatization of man's weakness before the power of the devil and his need for God's protection.

This need for God's protection is subtly developed in the third rhetorical unit, lines 32–50 (the storm at sea). Here the idea of the sea's war with the land is reintroduced (33–34) and elaborated (35b–39a). In the conflict of these huge enemies, the "dune" and the "oþer," man is reduced to terrifying insignificance, a creature with no hope except that implied in the closing question, "Hwa gestilleð þæt?"—a question calling for the answer given, as various scholars have pointed out, in Matthew 8:24–27, Christ's calming of the waves. In the fourth rhetorical unit, lines 51–81 (the thunderstorm on land), the demonology implied earlier is made explicit. The thunderclouds are dark, superhuman creatures (*earþan gesceafte,* 57b) warring as if with swords (57a), a great military troop (*atol eoredþreat,* 64a) of fire-hurling, thieving, devillike things from whom only God can save foolish man (68–73). The close of this rhetorical unit (74–81) focuses again on the contrast of the storm's seemingly limitless power and its dependence upon God's will. The poem's conclusion (82–89) reviews the three aspects of the storm and, like Riddle #1, asks an emotionally unanswerable question:

> Saga hwæt ic hatte,
> oþþe hwa mec rære,   þonne ic restan ne mot,
> oþþe hwa mec stæðþe,   þonne ic stille beom.

Is the question literal or allegorical or both? Does *rære* (88a) mean simply "rouse" or "elevate in station," "promote"? Does *stæðþe* (89a) mean "quiet" or "dignify"? Words like *hean* (84a) and *þeow* (82a), together with the poet's treatment, throughout the poem, of natural forces as retainers to God, urge us to answer, "Both." The physical view of natural forces, implied by the poet's use of the old cosmological books, and the superstitious view, implied by his treatment of the elements as "rynegiestas" (73b) or a "hloðgecrod" (78a), fuse in a quasi-mystical Christian view of the world as God's lawful and honorable (cf. *stæðþe*) dominion. By a controlled shifting of verbal contexts the poet has made the power of the storm emblematic of all forms of power, behind all of which stands the Lord.

Compared to the first of the storm riddles, the second is relatively explicit in its allegorizing of the central image, but even here we see that vertical allegory leaves some things to the reader's taste and judgment. In many riddles no decision whatever can be reached on whether or not allegory is present. In the swan riddle, for example, the central image is a traditional *figura* of the soul, and many details— the garments, the singing in the sky, etc.—make us suspect allegorical intent; but despite the consistency of details selected, and despite the absence of any detail contradicting the possible allegory, nothing here—not even "ferende gæst" (Riddle #7, line 9), since it is metaphoric—forces the listener beyond the literal. Debate over whether or not the poem is allegorical would be pointless, for the real point is that, here as in other riddles, verbal contexts shift, some phrases suggesting the idea of an angel (the singing, the wings as jewellike adornments: *hyrste,* 4a, and *frætwe,* 6b), some suggesting something human (1b–2), and all having metaphoric relationship to the swan.

Like the riddle poets, the authors of the *Physiologus* and *Phoenix* build up poetic texture in such a way as to force their literal material to carry allegorical overtones. No detailed stylistic analysis of these should be necessary, since their method is already well understood[8] and their poetic value, especially that of the *Phoenix,* generally acknowledged. Both poems of course close with interpretations of the images presented, but the listener need not hear the *significatio* to suspect that allegory is present in the images. Consider a brief example from the *Panther.*

> Þæt is wrætlic deor,   wundrum scyne
> hiwa gehwylces;   swa hæleð secgað,
> gæsthalge guman,   þætte Iosephes
> tunece wære   telga gehwylces
> bleom bregdende,   þara beorhtra gehwylc
> æghwæs ænlicra   oþrum lixte
> dryhta bearnum,   swa þæs deores hiw,
> blæc brigda gehwæs,   beorhtra ond scynra
> wundrum lixeð,   þætte wrætlicra
> æghwylc oþrum,   ænlicra gien
> ond fægerra   frætwum bliceð
> symle sellicra.

(19–30a)[9]

The rhetorical insistence on light and color makes a minor *kosmos* of the panther's hue and calls for interpretation. The allusion to Joseph's coat (typic of Christ's robe in exegetical commentary) calls up a religious context and points the direction of the allegory.

The same kind of rhetorical emphasis of certain details occurs in the *Phoenix*,[10] though more of this than has sometimes been recognized comes from the pseudo-Lactantian original. It is true that the poet's expansions of his source contribute to what Professor Greenfield has called "a symbolic density that only the best of its genre reveal,"[11] but the real beauty of this poem is not its density but the rhetorical ornamentation which fixes the listener's mind on the allegorical details. The poet repeatedly brings important images into the foreground of his poem by means of high-style rhetoric. This, for instance:

> Nis þær on þam londe   laðgeniðla,
> ne wop ne wracu,   weatacen nan,
> yldu ne yrmðu   ne se enga deað,
> ne lifes lyre,   ne laþes cyme,
> ne synn ne sacu   ne sarwracu,
> ne wædle gewin,   ne welan onsyn,
> ne sorg ne slæp   ne swar leger,
> ne wintergeweorp,   ne wedra gebregd,
> hreoh under heofonum,   ne se hearda forst,
> caldum cylegicelum,   cnyseð ænigne.
> þær ne hægl ne hrim   hreosað to foldan,
> ne windig wolcen,   ne þær wæter fealleþ,
> lyfte gebysgad,   ac þær lagustreamas,
> wundrum wrætlice,   wyllan onspringað
> fægrum flodwylmum.
>
> (50–64a)

When he comes to interpretation of the significance of such images, at the end of the poem, the poet echoes the rhetoric in which the images were presented. Thus at lines 611–14a, he writes:

> Ne bið him on þam wicum   wiht to sorge,
> wroht ne weþel   ne gewindagas,
> hungor se hata   ne se hearda þurst,
> yrmþu ne yldo.

The most spectacular instance of this is his echo of the passage on the phoenix and the sun (85–103, et passim) in his commentary on the soul as bird in the sun (583–601). In this rhetorical echoing, which can be matched in other poems of the Cynewulfian school (see discussion of *Elene,* Chapter 5), we have a curious variation on Caedmonic linear allegory, one used as ornamental reinforcement of vertical allegory.

If allegory like that in the *Phoenix* is cleverly managed, no closing explanation of the allegory is essential, at least in theory. In the *Wanderer* and its companion poem the *Seafarer* we have apparent applications of this principle. Though both poems were treated in earlier criticism as pagan poems with Christian interpolations and conclusions, more recent criticism is largely in agreement that the two elegies are unified structures exploring Christian themes—though critics are not in agreement on exactly what the poems mean.[12] The interest in both poems lies primarily in their deliberate ambiguity. In the *Seafarer,* as everyone knows, the same words used in different contexts suggest the contrast between the joys and companionship of this world and the joys of heaven (78–90) and between the protective power of an earthly ruler and that of God (39–43). (We have seen both contrasts developed in very similar terms in Caedmonic poems.) In the *Seafarer,* as in the riddles, double meanings reside in individual words, for instance the interpretative crux *elþeodigra eard,* which may mean a literal journey to foreign shores or may be a reference to heaven, true home of the exile in this world.[13] Again, the pivotal concept *hastening* (*onetteð,* 49b) looks two ways—"to the cyclical movement into springtime that is a call to travel, and to the movement of the world degeneratively toward its rendezvous with the millennium that is the added reason for the 'seafarer's' embarkation on his literal-allegorical journey to the only lasting security in heaven."[14] All this is of course familiar matter in *Wanderer* and *Seafarer* criticism. It will therefore be sufficient to note here that the verbal and imagistic ambiguity of the two poems is technically central, and that in moving from a primarily literal to a partly allegorical mode within the structure of each poem, the *Wanderer* and *Seafarer* poets introduce a variation on the technique of vertical allegory. The persona of each poem, clearly treated as literal as the poem begins, comes to be treated as both literal and allegorical, or, loosely, symbolic.

One might logically expect this technique to progress still further, to the presentation of the symbolic image alone, without explanation in a *significatio* or broadening toward allegory of the kind visible in the *Wanderer* and *Seafarer.* But here we encounter the same problem encountered in the riddle: when, in a short poem, a secular image or situation is developed in the mode of vertical allegory, and is not explicitly identified as allegorical, the allegory is unprovable; it can only be shown to be probable. Permit me to pause over a curious illustration of the difficulty.

Mixed in with the riddles in the Exeter Book we find the textually and otherwise baffling *Husband's Message*.[15] Manuscript holes make the opening all but unreadable; it is clear, however, that a tree is talking, that the tree has crossed "sealte streamas" on a ship, and that it comes bearing the husband's message. A similar association of tree and ship image occurs in Riddle #30, which F. A. Blackburn translated and explained as follows:

> I am agile of body, I sport with the breeze; [tree]
> I am clothed with beauty, a comrade of the storm; [tree]
> I am bound on a journey, consumed by fire; [ship, tree]
> A blooming grove, a burning gleed, [tree, log]
> Full often comrades pass me from hand to hand, [harp]
> Where stately men and women kiss me. [cup?]
> When I rise up, before me bow
> The proud with reverence. Thus it is my part
> To increase for many the growth of happiness. [the cross][16]

Discounting the identifications *harp* and *cup*, which most scholars reject for the more obvious solution, *cross*, this is certainly the right reading of the riddle. The connection between the tree, the ship, and the cross is emblematic, an equation of Noah's ship, adumbrative of the Church, and the cross. The same equation may be intended in the *Husband's Message*. With the introduction out of the way, the remainder of the *Husband's Message* slips easily into the exegete's grasp. The absent husband who gives out treasures across the sea is a figure of Christ the Bridegroom, and his message—have faith, trust our former vows—is the message of Christ to his traditionally widowed or separated wife, the Church. Nothing whatever in this poem resists exegetical interpretation, including the runes at the end. If we accept the reading of Hicketier, Bradley, and others, taking the *S* rune as *Sige* and keeping the other runes in their letter values *R EA W D*, i.e., *Sigeweard*, we have a likely designation of Christ.[17] No such consistent exegetical reading can be forced on *Deor, The Battle of Maldon, Widsith, Wulf and Eadwacer,* or the supposed companion piece to the *Husband's Message,* the *Wife's Lament,* despite the tempting oak tree and earth-cave in the *Lament*.

But we need not dwell on the difficulties involved in identifying all cases of vertical allegory. In this allegorical technique Anglo-Saxon poets found a new means of expression. Instead of versifying scriptural material, they could now explore secular images and situations in Christian terms. They had ready at hand virtually all the necessary stylistic devices for the writing of a poem like *Beowulf*—the Caedmonic device of rhythmic encoding, which could establish symbolic connections between events, and the techniques of vertical allegory which could turn Grendel, Grendel's mother, and the dragon into Christian-Platonic symbols of disorder. The same stylistic devices applied to another subject matter could turn a saint's life into an eschatological legend. Whether or not *Beowulf* actually came after the particular poems we have discussed as exemplifying part of its stylistic basis is of course not important for our purpose, nor is it important, though it is true, that Cynewulfian style, the logical culmination of the tradition, came late. What matters just here is the character of the stylistic elements. After linear and vertical allegory, Anglo-Saxon poets reached only one more important innovation, that which informs such poems as the Cynewulfian *Christ* and *Guthlac*.

Now let us turn to *Beowulf*.

4

Beowulf

The best of the Caedmonic poets went far beyond mere versification of biblical stories: they expanded, contracted, and, by rhythmic encoding, allegorized their material. The Christian riddle poets praised God not by retelling his Old and New Testament stories but by adapting the riddle to a Christian, quasi-allegorical purpose. The stylistic devices involved in this adaptive technique reached their highest expression, as we have seen, in poems like the *Physiologus*, the *Phoenix*, the *Wanderer*, and the *Seafarer*. All of these poems make Christian allegorical use of nonbiblical subject matter and thus reflect a shift of poetic concern, visible on the continent as well as in England, from the imitation of pagan eloquence to the borrowing of pagan material for a Christian purpose. Whereas the psychology of the Caedmonic poet results in rejection of pagan matter, the psychology of these poets allows comfortable acceptance of pagan matter and allegorical treatment of it. At its best—in *Beowulf*—this means allegory after the fashion of Virgil and others who "touched the truth and almost grasped it."

Both the linear and the vertical styles of allegory are present in *Beowulf*, as well as a third style on which I cannot conveniently comment until the end of Chapter 6, after I have discussed the Cynewulfian *Christ* trilogy. The linear style helps to shape the poem through echoes and repetitions: for instance, details from the "Lay of the Last Survivor" and the authorial comment following it (2247–70a) are repeated in the account of Hrethel's sorrow and the comparable sorrow of a man whose son has been hanged (2434–59). In the Lay we hear, for instance, "Næs hearpan wyn, gomen gleobeames . . ." (2262b–63a), and in the later passage, "nis þær hearpan sweg, gomen in geardum . . ." (2458–59a). The two passages are loaded with such parallels, and the poem, of course, has many such parallel passages. As for the vertical style of allegory, it may be seen in the poet's handling of his meadhall image, his three monsters, and other elements.

It will be best to begin not with the separate allegorical styles brought together in the poem but, instead, with the idea which organizes the poem as a whole, an idea based on the scheme of the tripartite soul.

Let me say at once that I am not much concerned about where the *Beowulf*-poet got his organizing idea. Fulgentius, much quoted and imitated down to Dante's time, is merely a likely source. When I speak of Fulgentius, I mean, in effect, Fulgentius, someone who had read Fulgentius, or someone whom Fulgentius had read.

Beowulf and the *Aeneid*

It is generally agreed, though not on very solid grounds, that the *Beowulf*-poet[1] knew Virgil's *Aeneid* or at least knew something about the *Aeneid*.[2] If he did, he must have understood the poem not as we do but as the best minds of his own age understood it, that is, as a poem valuable in part because it fulfilled medieval expectations of meaning beyond the literal. Virgil was "the divine pagan," and his epic was considered a poem susceptible of allegorical interpretation.[3] The most famous early interpretation was that of Fulgentius.

The *Expositio Vergiliana Continentia*[4]—much maligned and misunderstood in modern times—is a work designed, like the *Aeneid* itself in Fulgentius' view, both to delight and to instruct. (As I have said, earlier commentators may have offered a similar reading.)[5] As a dramatic frame for his sober exposition of one level of Virgil's allegory, Fulgentius casts his book in the form of a grim schoolroom exercise.[6] Struggling in vain over his subject, he calls for help so earnestly that he raises the ghost of Virgil himself, who appears not in his traditional smiling form but as a fierce old teacher who makes timid Fulgentius summarize Book I and who only then condescends to explain the epic to his student. Having asked to hear only the simplest of the expected three levels of allegory, Fulgentius learns only how the book treats the life of man. The key words, Virgil explains, are in the first line: *arma, virum,* and *primus.* The reader will need to see the Latin:

"arma," id est virtus, pertinet ad substantiam corporalem, "virum," id est sapientia, pertinet ad substantiam sensualem, "primus," vero, id est princeps, pertinet ad substantiam censualem, quo sit ordo huismodi: habere, regere, ornare. Ergo sub figuralitatem historiae plenum hominis monstrauimus statum, ut sit prima natura, secunda doctrina, tertia felicitas.[7]

Despite ambiguities in some key words, in Fulgentius' view of *arma, virum,* and *primus* one easily recognizes a preoccupation of early Church writers and of artists and poets down to the close of the Middle Ages: a concern with man's tripartite soul—rational, irascible, and concupiscent—analogous to the perfect three-part divine spirit, i.e., wisdom, power, goodness. The idea crops up everywhere, in explicit commentary on the soul, in treatments of the well-known "three temptations," and in casual discourse like which opens Lactantius' *Institutes.* Both pagans and Christians, Lactantius says, have pursued truth, "thinking it much more excellent to investigate and know the method of human and divine things [an activity of the rational soul], than to be entirely occupied with the heaping up of riches or the accumulation of honours [activities, respectively, of the concupiscent and irascible parts when they are not in proper subjugation to reason]."[8] Fulgentius is working with the same scheme when he explains in his *Mitologiarum* that the three goddesses among whom Paris must choose are symbols of the active (irascible), the contemplative (rational), and the amorous (concupiscent) life.[9] His identification of the three qualities of soul with three states of life, or ages, is a commonplace of medieval thought, though the parts of the soul and the ages of man are not always lined up in the same way. In the fourteenth-century *Parliament of the Three Ages,* for instance, youth is identified with the irascible part, middle ages with concupiscence, and old age with the search for wisdom.[10] In *Beowulf,* the basic Fulgentian scheme of the *Aeneid* reappears intact, with the important exception that the ending of *Beowulf* is tragic. Virgil does not deal with the decline and old age of his hero. The *Beowulf*-poet, influenced by Germanic and Christian ideas on the transcience of things, carries his poem beyond the hero's moment of *felicitas* to ambiguous victory and defeat.

Let us return to Fulgentius' explication of *arma, virum,* and *primus.* The first clause raises no difficulties: "arma" means any good quality, virtue, or moral excellence relating to things physical and informs the stage of *getting* (*habere*) in the life of man. *Arma,* in other words, means fortitude, valor, and the like—functions of the irascible soul in man. Virgil's *"virum,"* i.e., *wisdom* (*sapientia*), can only refer to what is intellectual—function of man's rational part—and informs the stage of *keeping what one has gotten (regere)*. Fulgentius' *"sensualem,"* then, has to do with *thought, understanding*; not *sensus* in the sense of *feeling*. It is *primus,* Fulgentius' *prince (princeps)*, that relates to the sensual and informs the stage of *adorning (ornare)* what one has gotten —a function of the well-ordered concupiscent soul. The word *censualem,* from *census,* has to do with fortune, estate, wealth, riches, fame. Comparetti, in his scornful summary of Fulgentius, reads "ornamental, artistic";[11] but he is interpreting, not translating. He is forcing a relationship between Fulgentius' words *censualem* and *ornare* and missing the true relationship: the amassing of wealth and fame (key ideas in *Beowulf*) are the adornment of the life of a good pagan. A later passage clarifies Fulgentius' meaning. *Primus* has to do with the proper use or enjoyment of things, Fulgentius says, and he quotes Plato: " 'Omne bonum aut nascitur aut eruditur aut cogitur'; nascitur guidem ex natura, eruditur ex doctrina, cogitur ex utilitate."[12] Fulgentius thus distinguishes between two kinds of wisdom: that which comes from teaching (erudition) and that which comes from reflection on the right use of things.

As he traces the story of Aeneas he shows that after man is freed from parental authority (the death and burial of Anchises), he first gives vent to unhealthy irascibility and concupiscence: man is overwhelmed by his passions (the storm) and seeks a false good (Dido). But instructed by intellect (Mercury) and the example of his father, he learns a nobler use of passion (the funeral games of Anchises). Freed from fantasies of good (Palinurus) and having put away vainglory (Misenus), he returns to instruction (the temple of Apollo). Armed with the golden branch (the knowledge which opens the way to hidden truths) he becomes a philosopher (the descent into Hades) and comes to understand the sorrows of life. Guided by time (Charon), he passes the troubled waters of youth (Acheron, earlier represented by Juno's storm, that is, birth), hears the quarrels and strifes that divide men (Cerberus' barking, earlier represented by the Cyclops at the end of Book III, whose one eye is emblematic of ignorance and quarrelsomeness), and sees quarrel stilled by the honey of wisdom. He comes to knowledge of the future life and to an understanding of good and evil, and he muses on the passions and affections of youth (Dido and Anchises). He is now free from instruction (the burial of Caieta) and reaches Ausonia, the increase of good. He takes labor as his mate (Lavinia) and allies himself with the good man (Evander) who shows him the triumph of virtue over crime (Hercules and Cacus). He makes himself a breastplate of his fiery spirit (Vulcan's arms), dashes into the struggle against anger (Turnus), drunkenness (Metiscus), obstinacy (Diuturna), impiety (Mexentius), and folly (Messapus). At last wisdom conquers all.

Concerned as he is with only the simplest of the allegorical levels in the *Aeneid,* Fulgentius does not say what the deeper levels are—though he clearly implies that deeper exegetical levels are present. Later tradition, reflected in the commentaries of Bernard of Chartres, John of Salisbury, and others[13]—and at some points anticipated in Lactantius and elsewhere—finds the *Aeneid* to be, on one level, an allegory of the soul's travel through the wilderness of life toward the New Jerusalem. Given the universal identification of Rome as the earthly center of God's kingdom, given Christ's role in opening the New Jerusalem, and given Dante's words on poetic allegory,[14] it is tempting to imagine that Aeneas may have been viewed very early as typic of Christ on the poem's eschatological level; but there are difficulties in the way of such a reading, perhaps the very difficulties which limited Fulgentius to the tropological level of the *Aeneid.* After the third-century condemnation of Origin, Christological interpretation of pagan figures (other than beasts, such as the phoenix) are uncommon. Anagogic readings of pagan fables remain uncommon until shortly before Boccaccio's time. Hercules is usually not considered as himself typic of Christ. Only in the "insular" Christian tradition—which survived in Ireland and may well have influenced the *Beowulf*-poet—did Christological allegory hold its own.[15]

The early Church argument was not that Virgil, Ovid, and the rest fully understood the allegories they presented. Unwittingly, they were "informed by the same spirit," the only possible source of inspiration. Two of Lactantius' remarks are worth mentioning for the light they may throw on *Beowulf.* Many pagans, he says, "however much they adorned the gods in their poems, and amplified their exploits with the highest praises, yet very frequently confess that all things are held together and governed by one spirit or mind."[16] He cites Orpheus, Maro, and Ovid, and elsewhere he often shows that Virgil was one of the fortunate. Further on in the *Institutes* he comments on the creation song of an unknown Sibyl, the details of which parallel those in the creation songs of Virgil's Iopas and the scop in Hrothgar's court: "But there is one only God of pre-eminent power who made the heaven, the sun, and stars, and moon, and fruitful earth, and waves of the water of the sea."[17]

Concerning the allegorizing of pagan fables, and particularly Virgil's fable of Aeneas, four points can be made. First, although many Christians may have valued pagan writing for its own sake—we recall, for instance, King Alfred's love of the old native songs and Bede's report of Aldhelm's skill as an oral poet on subjects both sacred and profane —the fact remains that the only established theoretical justification of pagan poetry (one Alfred and Aldhelm may have accepted) was that it carried Christian or at least moral instruction, literally, allegorically, or both. Second, the apparent pagan confusion concerning polytheism and monotheism was resolved in principle as early as the fourth century, though even by Boccaccio's time not all Christian writers accepted the standard resolution, namely, that the pagans in fact worshipped one god, though they gave god-names to his various attributes.[18] Third, where a pagan figure seems typic of Christ, he may be typic only in a limited way, as Klaeber pointed out:[19] he may prefigure Christ; he may or may not—like Christ-figures in some modern novels—directly represent him (Billy Budd, for instance). To complicate matters, the pagan figure may on one allegorical level pre-figure Christ and on another directly represent him. Recall the exegetical method. The first level ("literal," "grammatical," or "historical") says what is so: there was a man named Moses. On the "allegorical" or doctrinal level passages in the Old Testament prefigure events in the New. Extended to prerevelation pagan poetry, this means that Hercules' story, like Samson's, may prefigure Christ's (a point qualified above). On the "tropological" level, literal objects and events symbolically reveal moral principles. And on the "anagogical" level, literal objects and events become eschatological symbols. At least in theory, then, such figures as Aeneas and Beowulf might on the first two levels beyond the literal *prefigure* Christ and on the third directly represent him. As Klaeber showed, the connection need not be exact. If the pagan hero's life ends in failure, whereas Christ's ends in glorious triumph, that is no sure argument against typic identification. On the other hand, if the hero's life ends in triumph, that hero may nevertheless be only a human analogue. As we have said, Christological identification of a pagan figure is not historically probable outside the "insular" tradition but is at least possible within it. The fourth point to be noted is that if a seventh-century Christian poet and his audience knew any model at all for the Christian treatment of a pagan epic, that model was Virgil as men like Fulgentius understood him. Homer stood far below his Latin imitator, not only in the rhetoric books but in pious commentary as well.[20]

Before turning to parallels between *Beowulf* and Fulgentius' scheme, I must now insert a few preliminary remarks about this reading of *Beowulf*.

Preliminaries

We have no grounds for an a priori assumption that *Beowulf* is, as even Tolkien thought, a poem which has inconsistencies, not a "tight" work of art.[21] Its disjunctive and digressive nature is by no means proof of confusion or corruption by interpolation, as nearly all recent critics agree. The digressions make sense. Moreover, both in pre-Christian and in Christian poetry from Anglo-Saxon times we have instances of what might be called poetic mosaic, or, as some recent critics say, "interlace": that is to say, we find poems made up largely of old materials woven together for a new aesthetic purpose. Such interweaving, whether it was in fact Germanic or Christian in its origin, is at the heart of the period's rhetorical theory and has obvious analogues in Christian poetry in Latin.[22] We do have grounds, on the other hand, for a hypothesis that the poem is the systematic allegorization of pagan material, as such critics as McNamee and Nicholson maintain. If this hypothesis is right, we ought to be able to find the system complete, uncontradicted, and emphatic—that is, obvious, once we have the key. At the same time, once the consistent method has been made obvious, ingenious readings are legitimate if everything in the text supports them. Even startling reinterpretations of the text, like the head-spinning readings of Nicholson,[23] are acceptable if they are possible and if, more important, they make the poet's work coherent rather than self-contradictory.

At first glance it may seem that viewing *Beowulf* as partly an imitation of Virgil's method as understood by Fulgentius does not carry us far toward explaining away the references by pagan Danes to the creation or to Cain and Abel, or their seemingly Christian manner of speaking about God. Various solutions to these problems have been proposed;[24] I can add here only a footnote. Perhaps Cain's entrance into the poem can be accounted for in a way not yet suggested. The story seems not to be common knowledge among the Danes but the special knowledge of a professional collector and recounter of old stories: "*Sægde se þe cuþe*/frumsceaft fira feorran reccan . . ." (*Beowulf*, 90b–91; my italics). The story, moreover, is perhaps not, as commonly interpreted, one from far back in time but one "related from a distant place." Unless the present case is an exception, O. E. *feorran* involves space, not time.[25] The poetic license is that the story has come by oral transmission from the Hebrews to the Danes. Patristic arguments of pagan borrowing from Judaic tradition, together with the Middle Ages' bad geography and history, would support such a reading.[26] (The problem is complicated by the echoing passage at lines 1700 ff. where *feor* is as uncertain as *feorran*.)

The Danes' apparent knowledge of one God, though they worship many, presents no difficulty not resolved by Lactantius. Like Virgil and the rest, we must suppose, the Northern pagans had at very least a fitful and imperfect apprehension of the one true God. Some, like Hrothgar and Beowulf himself, had a clear and firm apprehension. The poet gives hints to his premise that the Christian God has always ruled, though not always recognized. For example:

> Ac him Dryhten forgeaf
> wigspeda gewiofu,   Wedera leodum,
> frofor ond fultum,   þæt hie feond heora
> ðurh anes cræft   ealle ofercomon,
> selfes mihtum.   Soð is gecyðed
> þæt mihtig God   manna cynnes
> weold wideferhð.

(696b–702a)

God has ruled mankind forever—all mankind, including those pagans whose knowledge of him was imperfect. It is for this reason that pagan experience, like Old Testament experience, can be searched for deeper significance in exactly the way pagan fables were studied down to the time of the *Gesta Romanorum* and beyond. In fact, it may be a hidden meaning of just this kind that prompts the *Beowulf*-poet's remark on God's long rule. In overcoming an enemy from the underworld for all the people, through his own power, Beowulf is analogous to Christ: he does for the Danes, within the physical domain of flesh-and-blood monsters, what Christ does in the spiritual domain when he overcomes the devil for all mankind. The analogy is frequently suggested —for instance when Beowulf's mother is singled out as, in effect, blessed among women.[27] If this is so, the poem reflects (as other evidence also hints) the insular Christian tradition—the tradition solidly established in East Anglia by men like St. Fursey. Insofar as the poem is anagogic, Beowulf is Christ; insofar as the poem involves simple "allegory" or tropology, Beowulf is a pagan prefiguration or analogue (ironic or straight) of Christ. In the interpretation I offer here—except near the end, where I cannot avoid invading his ground—I leave the dark woods of anagogy to Professor Nicholson, limiting myself to what Fulgentius slyly calls "the obvious."

In one important respect, the *Beowulf*-poet's identification of the Christian God and the Danes' chief god—the mysterious King, Measurer, Guardian, etc., mentioned throughout *Beowulf*—is fitting. *Wul-dor-cyning* is consistently viewed, here as in Caedmonic verse, as a ruler analogous to earthly rulers; his code of behavior is directly analogous to the code of any Germanic earthly ruler who is wise and good. The heroic ethic, rational law in its Northern form, is the earthly counterpart of divine Law. As the good Germanic chieftain pays his retainers for worthy service, so God pays men. The difference, central to the poem's meaning, is that the earthly king works within the intransigent limits of mutability: all things physical are doomed.

The poet's main symbol of the doomed world of things physical is the meadhall, where—he insists by verbal repetition—sleep comes after the feast: allegorically, the sleep of death which succeeds the feast of life. This metaphor is urged at many points, perhaps also in the name of Hrothgar's hall, "Hart" (also, of course, "heart"). While the name fits the horn-curving appearance of the hall, it also recalls for the Christian audience one of Isaiah's chief symbols of the world to be destroyed in the great destruction he foretells, the hart which dragons will devour—a symbol common in medieval Church representations of the end of the world—on columns and panels as well as liturgy and sermon.[28]

This identification of the meadhall and the world explains several otherwise obscure passages. This, for instance:

> Wæs þæt beorhte bold   tobrocen swiðe
> eal inneweard   irenbendum fæst,
> heorras tohlidene;   hrof ana genæs
> ealles ansund,   þe se aglæca
> fyrendædum fag   on fleam gewand,
> aldres orwena.   No þæt yðe byð
> to befleonne   —fremme se þe wille—,
> ac gesecan sceal   sawlberendra
> nyde genydde,   nipða bearna,
> grundbuendra   gearwe stowe,
> þær his lichoma   legerbedde fæst
> swefeþ æfter symle.
>
> (997–1008a)

Perhaps on the level of allegory, the roof of Hart is spared because in the destruction of the world the upper region, heaven, will remain. But this reading cannot be pushed very far; for eventually the whole of Hart will burn, so that if any allegory is intended here, it is local and momentary. The lines which come next are more puzzling and more important. Grendel seeks to flee the meadhall but finds it difficult,[29] for though he may escape the literal meadhall, all around him lies the larger (allegorical) meadhall where, however he may struggle to escape, he and all things mortal (*fremme se þe wille*) . . . *swefeþ æfter symle.* (Cf. 119a, *swefan æfter symble.*) The world is the hall through which the sparrow flies from darkness to darkness.

The same metaphor explains the much debated lines on Grendel and the *gifstol.*

> Heorot eardode,
> sincfage sel   sweartum nihtum;—
> no he þone gifstol   gretan moste,
> maþðum for Metode,   ne his myne wisse.
>
> (166b–69)

Grendel can occupy the literal meadhall, Hart, but as a creature eternally exiled from God's favor, he can never "know his desire" in the cosmic meadhall, or approach the treasure-throne of God.[30] It is not only Hrothgar's but this sorrow as well that the poet means by his squinting phrase, "þaet waes wraec micel. . . ."[31] The listener at first takes the phrase to refer to the oft-mentioned sorrow of Grendel (a closing commentary phrase parallel to *þaet waes god cyning*). Then finding that the phrase leads to *wine Scyldinga,* the listener intuits the comparison, made explicit at lines 183b–88, between the everlasting sorrow of the outcast sinner (Grendel) and the temporary sorrow of the tested faithful man (typified by Hrothgar). The Danes, who when they went to sleep *sorge ne cuðon* (119b) and who, later, came to know grief, were better off at least than the *wiht unhaelo* ("miserable creature," even "creature unsaved") whose grief was permanent, as the Christian poet and his audience are in a position to understand. This, I am suggesting, is the contrast pointed up for that audience—a contrast which would be meaningless to those who followed the pagan *þeaw* (178b)—between those who suffer forever for their sins and those who, whatever their troubles in this world, may come eventually to bliss:

> Wa bið þæm ðe sceal
> þurh sliðne nið   sawle bescufan
> in fyres fæþm,   frofre ne wenan,
> wihte gewendan!   Wel bið þæm þe mot
> æfter deaðdæge   Drihten secean
> ond to Fæder fæþmum   freoðo wilnian!
>
> (183b–88)

God, like a wise earthly chieftain, protects the good—Scyld, for instance, who after a bad beginning, "frofre gebad," or Hrothgar who, after hard times, is sent Beowulf as a help and comfort. Hrothgar has been expecting some such help as this, he tells Wulfgar—"þæs ic wen hæbbe" (383b)—for he has never lost faith in the cosmic ruler's justice. Those unfaithful to God, on the other hand, "frofre ne wenan" (185b) exactly as those snatched by Grendel, typic of the fiend, "ne . . . wenan þorfte / beorhte bote to banan folmum" (157b–58).

In *Beowulf,* in short, God is consistently presented as the ruling god of Northern pagans in that, first, he is God as understood before the Incarnation (his gift of life after death is not yet known) and, second, he is the model of the ideal Germanic chieftain, Guardian of the Hall. The central irony in the poem, and the basis of its tragic conclusion, is that, prior to the full revelation of God's plan, the heroic ethic by which God works does not visibly operate on earth, where it seems that no man is finally paid as he deserves because all men die. The best one can hope for is lasting "dom," a word which means one thing to the pagan, another thing—more joyful—to the Christian.

What, you may ask, has all this to do with Fulgentius' *arma, virum,* and *primus?*

Professor Leyerle, like Professor Kaske, has insisted upon the central importance in Beowulf of Hrothgar's words to Beowulf on pride.[32]

> Wundor is to secganne
> hu mihtig God   manna cynne
> þurh sidne sefan   snyttru bryttað,
> eard ond eorlscipe;   he ah ealra geweald.
> Hwilum he on lufan   læteð hworfan
> monnes modgeþonc   mæran cynnes,
> seleð him on eþle   eorðan wynne
> to healdanne,   hleoburh wera,
> gedeð him swa gewealdene   worolde dælas,
> side rice,   þæt he his selfa ne mæg
> for his unsnyttrum   ende geþencean.
> Wunað he on wiste;   no hine wiht dweleð
> adl ne yldo,   ne him inwitsorh
> on sefa(n) sweorceð,   ne gesacu ohwær
> ecghete eoweð,   ac him eal worold
> wendeð on willan   he þæt wyrse no con—,
> oðþæt him on innan   oferhygda dæl
> weaxeð ond wridað.   þonne se weard swefeð,
> sawele hyrde;   bið se slæp to fæst,
> bisgum gebunden,   bona swiðe neah,

se þe of flanbogan   fyrenum sceoteð.
þonne bio on hreþre   under helm drepen
biteran stræle   —him bebeorgan ne con—,
wom wundorbebodum   wergan gastes;
þinceð him to lytel   þæt he lange heold,
gystað gromhydig,   nallas on gylp seleð
fætte beagas,   ond he þa forðgesceaft
forgyteð ond forgymeð,   þæs þe him ær God sealde,
wuldres waldend,   weorðmynda dæl.

(1724b–52)

Close reading of these lines—and a test of this reading against the rest of the poem—shows that whereas Fulgentius overreads pagan statements, discovering in them more meaning than is there, the *Beowulf*-poet extends old Germanic ideas, making pagan speakers say more than they know how to mean. The pagans knew the difference between selfishness and selflessness and understood the wrongness of selfish pride like Heremod's; but certainly Hrothgar could not know the theory of the tripartite soul, the basis of his reasoning to Beowulf. According to Hrothgar, God gives man wisdom, land (i.e., possession), and *eorlscipe* (i.e., manliness, bravery, courage). God gives, in other words, those things which pertain to the rational, concupiscent, and irascible parts of the soul (following Hrothgar's ordering of elements). If this seems at first an overreading, the sense of the lines which follow is unmistakable. When things go well for a man for a long time, his *weard*—his rational part—may fall asleep. A murderer very close to him, inside him in fact, prompted by the devil, strikes. As did Heremod, the man becomes angry-hearted (the malfunctioning irascible part having seized command) and covetous (a malfunction of the concupiscent soul). What happens next, from Hrothgar's pagan point of view—for the poet has given him the Christian-Platonic system, but not revelation—is that the proud man grows old and weak, and (possibly murdered, like Heremod, for his cruelty and stinginess) he dies. To the Christian audience, Hrothgar's statements have a broader meaning: failing in wisdom, sinking to sinful wrath and covetousness, man dies to the life hereafter. The symbolism of the meadhall has of course been inverted—or extended: what stood, before, for the macrocosm now stands for the microcosm as well. As the hall is guarded (e.g., by Hrothgar), a man is guarded by his rational part. As the hall may be attacked by a monster (e.g., Grendel) when the guardian trusts too much in himself (cf. 1769 ff.), a man may be overcome by pride, an effect of the irascible and concupiscent souls' tyranny over the rational.

Hrothgar of course fares better in the analogy than does Heremod. His trust in God's justice and control brings Beowulf.

This idea of tragic fall through pride is developed in the poem in three ways. In the sphere of private morality, the life of Beowulf moves through *arma* (Professor Kaske's "fortitudo") to *virum, id est sapientia* (as Professor Kaske saw)[33] toward Fulgentius' *primus,* a stage Beowulf the man perhaps tragically misses because, accustomed to success in battle, he fails to take his army with him to fight the dragon—in other words because, if John Leyerle's interpretation of the poem is even partly right,[34] Beowulf's *virum* gave way: *se weard swefeð.* In the sphere of social morality, the fall of the Danes and the impending fall of the Geats is explained as a partial failure of wisdom and valor. On the poem's cosmic level, the three focal monsters are figures of perverted rationality, perverted irascibility, and a double perversion, irascible and concupiscent. The general relevance of Fulgentius' scheme to the meaning of *Beowulf* is not difficult to show. More specific parallels, for example a possible relationship between Unferth (or *discordia*)[35] and the Cyclops, may also be present, but they are impossible to prove.

The First Movement: Beowulf and Grendel

In the opening section of *Beowulf* the poet sets up the terms of the heroic ethic (Fulgentius' principles of felicity); then, as Virgil shows Aeneas' education, the *Beowulf*-poet shows, through allusions to the hero's past, how Beowulf came to his present maturity, the unambiguous state of wisdom and valor from which, in his last days, he will decline. It will be necessary to trace this process.

The first section of *Beowulf*—lines 1–52, concerning the life and death of Scyld—might not be altogether necessary as background information for the story of Beowulf the Geat. The poet might have begun with Hrothgar; or if historical background were his sole concern, he might have begun before the break in the line of Danish monarchy, that is, before Scyld's arrival. He may have wanted the formal balance of Beowulf's funeral and Scyld's, but there is every indication that the poet had also another, more central purpose. The whole focus of his treatment is on reward or payment within the heroic ethic, reward for three kinds of virtue. Scyld, who began as a foundling, destitute,[36] eventually received *frofre* for that (7b), and the Danes, lordless before Scyld's rise to power, receive *frofre* (14a) in the birth of Scyld's son. In a moralizing intrusion the poet claims that Beow's generosity to his retainers while his father still rules is praiseworthy because it will win the retainers' later loyalty. (Beow; in older readings, Beowulf the Dane.) The promise of the heroic ethic (later revealed to be unsure in the human sphere) is that "lof daedum sceal / in mægþa gehwære man geþeon." Finally, the gifts placed on the dead Scyld's ship show in another way that virtue is rewarded.

Scyld's line descends to Hrothgar, and the poet turns to that king's building of his meadhall, to Grendel's attacks, and to the dreadful time of sorrow endured by the king in his old age. Hrothgar is the dramatic center of the poem's first movement: all that comes before points forward to him and defines his condition; all that comes later recalls and clarifies his condition. *Beowulf* begins and ends with the sorrows of an old man.

Having been given power in battle, Hrothgar builds the hall to dispense the treasures he has won and also to increase his fame—the hall is to be known throughout earth. This passage in the poem (53–85) reinforces ideas in the first passage and helps to crystallize them. The controlling ideas can be reduced to the formula *arma, virum, primus*. Through *arma*, Scyld and the rest come to deserve God's pay; through *virum*—wise rule, which involves paying others as God has paid them —good kings like Beow maintain their power; and the adornment of that power is their fame as noble kings of a mighty nation, their collection of tribute, or their building of some great hall for the just disposition of treasures. Scyld comes to *weorðmyndum* (8b); Beow "wæs breme—blæd wide sprang" (18). To dispense the treasures which have come with his prowess, Hrothgar builds Hart.

But now Grendel arrives on the scene (86–193), tormenting a brave and generous king who deserves only good, and it begins to appear that the promise of the heroic ethic was vain. This is no new note. Scyld vanished into the "realm" of the "garsecg," and no man (neither the courageous nor the wise, neither *seleraedende* nor *haele under heofenum*) knows "who received that cargo."[37] (The poet himself is, of course, not so pessimistic. Scyld went "into the protection of the Lord.") Other ominous details have been presented. The poet's words on the glory of Hart were at once undercut, as Bonjour pointed out,[38] by a prophecy of the hall's destruction. Now, in Grendel, the poet presents the *loser* in that ethic by which winners like Scyld, through their mighty deeds and wisdom, win *frofre*.

The focus of the lines introducing Grendel is on the monster's sorrowing rage. He feels envy and spite, and the cause is "þæt he dogora gehwam dream gehyrde / hludne in healle . . ." (88–89a). Perhaps the joy of the Danes would be sufficient alone to infuriate this creature of anguish, but the scop's song, which recalls the time when Grendel's suffering had its beginning, makes things worse. As Hrothgar in his triumph created and adorned Hart, God in His triumph made the world. The scop tells of God's adorning of the plains, an image which, supported by *repetitio* (*frætwan*, 76a, *gefrætwade*, 96a), recalls the adorning of the meadhall; and the scop tells how God set out the sun and moon as signs of victory, recalling the fact that Hrothgar built his hall to share his battle winnings when he was *heresped gyfen* (64). God's victory signs are *leoman to leohte, landbuendum;* of Hart the poet will later say, "lixte se leoma," "ofer landa fela" (95 and 311). God's first victory, presumably, was a victory over chaos (so both Christian and Northern tradition would have it), but he soon won another which caused Grendel's sorrow. When Cain murdered Abel, "feuding" with God and setting off the long war of God and the monsters, he won exile and darkness for all his line. In his comment, "he him ðæs lean forgeald," (114b) the poet ironically contrasts the reward of the kind Scyld got for his worthy deeds and the grim reward God gave Cain for what was, in effect, his wicked perversion of *arma*. (The reference in 114b may not be to the flood, which takes place later than Beowulf's time, but simply to God's decree of eternal exile for Cain and his line. Either reading will do.)

The lines on Hrothgar's misery after Grendel's first attack further elaborate the Caedmonic analogy between God's meadhall and that of an earthly king. The poet ironically compares the sorrows brought about by the monster to the sorrow brought about by a brooding thane in a hall.

> Þa wæs eaðfynde   þe him elles hwær
> gerumlicor   ræste [sohte],
> bed æfter burum,   ða him gebeacnod wæs,
> gesægd soðlice   sweotolan tacne
> healðegnes hete;   heold hyne syðþan
> fyr ond fæstor   se þæm feonde ætwand.
>
> (138–43)

Later incidents in the poem suggest that the common interpretation of "healðegnes hete" as "the hatred of him who now controlled the hall" (Donaldson's translation[39]) is wrong. O. E. *þegn* normally means "servant, warrior, one who dwells in the hall," not ruler. The lines involve a typically grim Anglo-Saxon joke. Grendel's all too obvious hatred of the hall, revealed by the "clear tokens" of mangled corpses and smashed tables is ironically compared with the secret hostility of a retainer who bears a grudge which he reveals by subtle but unmistakable signs. It was no doubt relatively common in ancient Germania (as it is in *Beowulf*) to find a court thrown into confusion and bloodshed by a man who had for a long time clenched his teeth against his anger at those around him. Just as a retainer who catches on to the secret hostility of the Hengest beside him on the bench may discreetly keep out of the angry man's way, so Hrothgar's retainers give a wide berth to Grendel. If this reading at first seems difficult, notice the heavy irony in the poet's language throughout the passage just quoted. The word *eaðfynde* grimly understates the real situation: it is in fact virtually impossible to find a Dane who will remain all night in Hart. The dark joke has a point. It looks forward to a central concern of the second movement of *Beowulf,* the disorder which erupts when, despite Hoc's gift of Hildeburh as a "peace-weaver," one of Finn's men will turn on one of Hnaef's (as later Hengest will turn on Finn), or the disorder which will erupt to ruin Hart. Both valor and wise rule may prove untrustworthy. The *arma* of such men as Scyld win payment from God, just as Beowulf's valor will win payment from Hrothgar; but as Cain's crimes show, as Grendel's spite proves, and as Grendel's mother's rage will also show, courage and loyalty have their black side: lawless blood-revenge; that is, *arma* gone mad. The valor of the noble Hengest results in slaughter.

But in the first movement of the poem, the poet drops ony dark hints of all this. His emphasis is on the nature of the heroic life as systematized by Fulgentius' scheme for the *Aeneid:* how brave deeds result in "getting," how a good king's grasp of the code (*virum, sapientia*) should lead to "keeping," and how this should lead to wealth and fame (*primus*) and the adorning of that rule (*ornare*).

The poet dwells now on Hrothgar's misery and by epithets praising the old Danish king's valor and wisdom insists on the shocking unnaturalness of Hrothgar's situation. What seems most terrible about it is that nothing can be done; Grendel's feud with man has no law. Whereas normally a man might buy off his enemy by gifts of tribute of the kind sent to Scyld and later to Hrothgar, and whereas normally Germanic law would provide at least the satisfaction of *wergild,* in the case of Grendel there seems no hope. Grendel is a creature of *sinnihte,* perpetual night, in a Boethian sense; he is a *helruna*—literally, a "counsellor in hell,"[40] which is as much as to say, one who denies law and reason at their source.

The lines alluding to *Daniel* moralize the dissimilar sorrows of Hrothgar and Grendel.

> þæt wæs wraec micel   wine Scyldinga,
> modes brecða;   monig oft gesæt
> rice to rune;   ræd eahtedon,
> hwæt swiðferhðum   selest wære
> wið færgryrum   to gefremmanne.
> Hwilum hie geheton   æt hærgtrafum
> wigweorþunga,   wordum bædon,
> þæt him gastbona   geoce gefremede
> wið þeodþreaum.   Swycl wæs þeaw hyra,
> hæþenra hyht;   helle gemundon
> in modsefan,   Metod hie ne cuþon,
> dæda Demend,   ne wiston hie Drihten God,
> ne hie huru heofena Helm   herian ne cuþon,
> wuldres Waldend.   Wa bið þæm ðe sceal
> þurh sliðne nið   sawle bescufan
> in fyres fæþm,   frofre ne wenan,
> wihte gewendan!   Wel bið þæm þe mot
> æfter deaðdæge   Drihten secean
> ond to Fæder fæþmum   freoðo wilnian!
>
> (170–88)

These lines are among the most difficult in the poem, admittedly—difficult precisely because they may mean different things on different levels of allegory. If Beowulf is viewed as a straight Christ-figure (as he aways is in Nicholson's readings) and the Danes are viewed as holy pagans directly equivalent to the theologically well-informed Old Testament Jews to whom Christ came, the lines treat real backsliding. But if the lines are read as treating things "more obvious"—theologically uninformed Danes whose intuition of the one wuldor-cyning is not solid enough to protect them from panic—Hrothgar's men are not real backsliders but only men whose moral situation can be illuminated by allusion to the dissimilar situation of Belshazzar's court.

It is to discover a defense against *færgryrum* (attacks of terror, not terrible attacks) that Hrothgar's counsellors meet. Hrothgar's precise concern, in other words, is the *fear* which has depopulated his hall—that is, it is the effect of Grendel's onslaughts. Knowing no better way to rebuild courage (*arma*), lacking the true wisdom of a Christian (*virum*), the Danes mistakenly seek support from idols. What they do by the dim light of "þeaw hyra," though not truly wise, is not to be condemned; but the allusion to that passage in *Daniel* wherein people

who *did* know about God turned their backs on Him implies a comparison between the God-defying Grendel and any in the Christian
audience who incline (as did King Raedwald's wife and Eorpwald's
court in East Anglia)[41] toward Belshazzar's mistake. If the Danes
helle gemundon for lack of instruction and for lack of stubborn faith,
like Hrothgar's, in the cosmic Chieftain's justice, Grendel and the
backslider turn against God in dangerous error, forgetting that God in
his dual role as ruler, Drihten (181b), and righteous Measurer, Metod
(180b)—aspects of *virum,* regulating wisdom—can overwhelm the
violence which breeds panic (two failures of *arma*). The phrase *sliðne
nið* refers to the sorrows and hostile feelings of Grendel and also the
backslider; it also (as a pun)[42] suggests the dreadful effects of graven
images.

The scheme of valor, wisdom, and reward set up in the poem thus
far leads us to expect some comfort for Hrothgar. It comes in the form
of Beowulf the Geat, the strongest man in the world. The poem now
becomes Beowulf's poem—the story of his maturation and ambiguous
final victory. In his dealings with the Danes he shows wisdom equal
to Hrothgar's and valor beyond that which, long ago, gave Hrothgar
might in battle.

What is central in the drama of Beowulf's expedition to Hart is
the awkwardness of the situation and Beowulf's skill in handling it.
He is, quite simply, a superman among very strong men—a walking
icon of *arma*. His wisdom and tact make him an icon of *virum*. He
cuts a fine figure, sailing off with his hand-picked fourteen, but his
very glory is an embarrassment to the Danes, as Beowulf knows. He
tells the coastguard,

> Habbað we to þæm mæran   micel ærende
> Deniga frean;   ne sceal þær dyrne sum
> wesan, þæs ic wene.   Þu wast gif hit is
> swa we soþlice   secgan hyrdon. . . .
>
> (270–73)

He dislikes speaking of the matter so shameful to the Danish retainers, and he carefully avoids saying he has come to do by his
valor what they could not; he says he comes to give advice "þurh
rumne sefan" (278a).[43] The coastguard of Hrothgar's weakened kingdom answers subtly: "A man who thinks well must judge of two
things, words and works." He means that the seeming offense in Beowulf's bold landing is cancelled by his friendly words; but he may

also mean, "We shall see, Beowulf, whether your works match your words," that is "whether you have *arma* as well as *virum*."

The Geats march up toward Hart, and the poet shifts his vantage point so that the listener sees them coming as the Danes do. The selection of details tells the story: glittering boarhelmets, singing armor, bright weapons. As the coastguard noted the Geats' ominously bold landing, Wulfgar comments immediately on their warlike dress and bearing (333 sq.), and when he speaks of his lord it is with a respect that emphasizes Hrothgar's worth as a ruler (*virum*): in six lines he calls Hrothgar "wine Deniga," "frean Scildinga," "beaga bryttan," "þeoden mærne," and "se goda" (350b–55). Hrothgar's fitness to rule is not exaggerated. When Wulfgar carries the Geats' message to the king, Hrothgar eases the Danish thanes' situation. He makes a point—for the benefit of the warriors around him—of how he knew Beowulf as a boy; he mentions the long-standing friendship of the Danes and Geats (the Danes have sent gifts "to þance"); and he attributes Beowulf's coming not to Beowulf's courage and might— though these must certainly be in his mind—but to God's mercy.

Now Beowulf must present his credentials, an awkward situation, since all he must say will seem vainglorious to the Danes. But Beowulf speaks well, with as much discernment and discretion as Hrothgar himsef could show (407–55). He presents himself as Hygelac's man (not a glory seeker) and seems to dismiss the great deeds of his youth with a general allusion to "mærða fela" (408b). Not his own pride but the advice of "snotere ceorlas" (416b) has sent him here; and it is by way of explaining the wise men's choice that he mentions his specific feats. Since Grendel scorns weapons, Beowulf will fight bare-handed, not from personal pride (a perversion of *virum*) but in order to give Hygelac pleasure and honor (435b–36), as is fitting. He ends with grim jokes on how cheaply Hrothgar will get off if Grendel wins (jokes grounded on the *primus, ornare* theme). Hrothgar supplements Beowulf's words: "For [g]ewy[r]htum þu, wine min Beowulf, / ond for arstafum (past favors) usic sohtest" (457–58). (Klaeber's emendation is perhaps too bold.) In other words, according to Hrothgar Beowulf comes partly in obedience to duty; and Hrothgar tells of the time he helped Beowulf's father. As Beowulf minimized his own role, no doubt sincerely, by giving the outcome of the proposed battle to God (440b–41) and Fate (455), Hrothgar says, "God eaþe mæg / þone dolsceaðon dæda getwæfan!" (478–79). Finally, Hrothgar reminds the Danes of their own failure to back their words with works (480 sq.).

Now Unferth, official wrangler—a "þyle," or trouble-making priest

of Woden[44]—one of those heroes whose honor is most directly threatened by the Geat, launches his verbal attack. He enters the poem
primarily as a foil to Beowulf's *virum:* Unferth is mistaken in his facts,
is motivated by wrath and (to the Christian audience) erroneous religion, and is drunk. In other words his reasoning is ill-grounded, and
his irascible and concupiscent souls are faulty. Unferth makes, and
Beowulf responds to, two main points: (1) the swimming match with
Breca was stupid vainglory, and (2) Breca won, proving Beowulf
second-rate, a man of mere words. He makes his first point brilliantly,
beginning with an incredulous, loaded question:

> "Eart þu se Beowulf,   se þe wið Brecan wunne,
> on sidne sæ   ymb sund flite,
> ðær git for wlence   wada cunnedon
> ond for dolgilpe   on deop wæter
> aldrum neþdon?   Ne ince ænig mon,
> ne leof ne lað,   belean mihte
> sorhfullne sið,   þa git on sund reon; . . .

$$(506-12)$$

They swam, Unferth says, "for wlence" and "for dolgilpe," that is, for
pride and because of a stupid boast; and they would take advice from
no man. This is the third reference to the idea of taking advice before
an act of daring: clearly, getting advice is of some importance. Beowulf
got wise men's approval of his journey to Hart, the poet mentions
(202–3), and Beowulf himself has reported this to Hrothgar (415–18).
The poet's repetitions of the advice motif suggest that Unferth may be
right in saying Beowulf would listen to no one at the time of the
match with Breca. He is wrong about Breca's winning, and Beowulf
easily answers the charge, but Beowulf gives no direct answer to the
charge that he acted like a fool. He admits that the match was the
behavior of mere boys, of whom *virum* presumably should not be
demanded (535–38), and grants that it is perhaps nothing to be especially proud of: "no ic þæs [fela] gylpe" (586b). But he does have a
negative defense, one implicit in his first words to Unferth: "Hwæt,
þu worn fela, wine min Unferð, / beore druncen, ymb Brecan
spræce . . ." (530–31). He is of course echoing Hrothgar's complaint
about empty words, "Ful oft gebeotedon, beore druncne" (480), and
thus suggesting two things at once: that Unferth's version of the
swimming match is empty language, like the boasts of the warriors
who proved weak, and that Unferth himself is a talker, not a fighter.

Though Beowulf acknowledges that he may once have acted boyishly, he denies that he ever lacked selflessness or valor. If Unferth were braver, Grendel would be dead. He adds, suddenly cutting deep, that the only act of bravery he can call to mind in connection with Unferth's name is perverted valor (like Cain's), the murder of kinsmen. Though Beowulf as a young man may have possessed more valor than wisdom, the monsters he killed were a trouble to the Geats. He understands now, if he did not then, that valor means service (the point of the advice motif), not derring-do for its own sake. It is because valor serves that it wins payment in the heroic ethic. In his battle of words he turns his knowledge against his opponent and defeats him; and in his next boast, to Wealtheow (632–38), he again shows his command of the ethic. *Virum:* in the company of his "secga gedriht," he says, he resolved to do the will (or pleasure) of the Danish people. (He rules himself and knows his place as defender of order.) *Arma:* he claims himself no weaker than Grendel and in fairness renounces weapons because Grendel knows no weapons. And *primus:* he leaves the outcome—the payment, good or bad—to God's judgment. And so, mature in what Fulgentius calls *virum,* and clear about valor's implications both with respect to those served and with respect to enemies, Beowulf fights Grendel and wins. In sign of victory, the Danes have horse races, the scop sings a song, and Hrothgar comes out with Wealtheow and her attendants to give thanks to God and praise the hero. Hart is renovated and once again adorned, and Beowulf receives the generous payment he has earned.

The closing section of what I have called the first of the three movements of *Beowulf*[45] shows the larger implications of the heroic ethic and at the same time sets up the central concern of the poem's next movement—the darker side of the ethic. Section XVI opens with a bald statement, by the poet himself, of the relationship between wisdom and courage, and an explanation of why the brave and wise do not always prosper.

Beowulf has just been given gifts. Now the poet says:

> Ða gyt æghwylcum   eorla drihten
> þara þe mid Beowulfe   brimlade teah,
> on þære medubence   maþðum gesealde,
> yrfelafe,   ond þone ænne heht
> golde forgyldan,   þone ðe Grendel ær
> mane acwealde,—   swa he hyra ma wolde,
> nefne him witig God   wyrd forstode
> ond ðæs mannes mod.   Metod eallus weold
> gumena cynnes,   swa he nu git deð.

Forþan bið andgit   æghwær selest,
ferhðes foreþanc.   Fela sceal gebidan
leofes ond laþes   se þe longe her
on ðyssum windagum   worolde bruceð!

(1050–62)

Grendel was stopped from killing more by two things, wise God and the valor of Beowulf. But that explanation can be refined, the next lines show. *Metod,* that is, God the Measurer, or Wisdom, has always ruled men. It is for this reason (*Forþan*—not in an adversative sense) that discernment is everywhere best: only in a reasonable, ordered universe does *andgit* count. Thus Grendel was beaten not only by the valor of Beowulf but also by the wisdom of Beowulf and, more centrally, Hrothgar, who waited out his time of troubles and kept his faith that God would send payment. It is the nature of the world that man must experience both the good and the bad; but *ferhðes foreþanc,* another form of Fulgentius' *virum* or sapience, can be trusted.

The scop's song, if we accept one standard reconstruction, immediately casts doubt on that theory. For reasons the poet's original audience fully understood, probably some old "sword-grudge," Hoc's forethought—his attempt to avoid war by giving his daughter to the man threatening him—was of no avail: despite Hildeburh, Finn's Frisians turned on Hnaef and murdered him; and despite Finn's reasonable peace terms—that no man should either by words or works break the truce or complain at serving his lord's murderer, Hengest can no more contain his grief forever than winter can forever keep Hengest from his homeland. Both Hoc and Finn, in other words, tried to check social passion (love of the murdered friend and hunger for revenge) by wisdom, the rational system of fair payment which is basic to the heroic ethic.[46] Both rulers failed. So too the faith Hrothgar and Wealtheow place in reason will fail to save Hart. Wealtheow hopes that, just as the generosity of Beow (the Dane) made his men faithful later, the generosity of her house to Hrothgar's nephew Hrothulf will win his later loyalty to her son. It may not. Neither will Hrothgar's gift of his daughter to Ingeld bring any lasting peace. By the same rules that it saves a man, the heroic ethic can destroy him, for the end of that ethic is not order (Hrothgar's kind of glory) but a more selfish personal glory, the common Anglo-Saxon idea of felicity, a perversion of Fulgentius' *primus.* This is the subject of the second movement of *Beowulf,* where the idea summed up in Fulgentius' *virum* is further qualified by dramatic exploration of what is implied, for the pagan and for the Christian, in the idea of *primus.*

The Second Movement: Beowulf and Grendel's Dam

The second movement begins with a curious summary of material from the first movement. The unexpected attack of a second monster prompts the poet to speak again of the first, of Cain's exile, and of Beowulf's victory, and thus allows him to reinforce his meaning by repetition.

Like all we have heard before of Grendel, every statement here insists on his character as cosmic outlaw. He was, earlier, a "hell-counsellor," guilty of "crimes" and "sins," one who "warred against right." We now hear how he "unriht æfnde, oþ þæt ende becwom, swylt æfter synnum" (1254–55b). Grendel's mother is also of the tribe of Cain, but nothing is said of her crimes or sins.[47] She lives in misery in terrible, cold streams because of the deeds of the outlaw Cain, but she is presented not as an enemy of right but as an avenger. The central importance of vengeance in this movement explains why Grendel's dam kills not merely some unnamed warrior but one of Hrothgar's most dearly beloved retainers, Aeschere, Yrmenlaf's brother. Both Aeschere's lord and Aeschere's faithful warriors—those who looked to him as their treasure-giver—must now cry out for vengeance. The heroic bargain has gone awry. As the poet says, "Ne wæs þæt gewrixle til, / þæt hie on ba healfa bicgan scoldon / freonda feorum!" (1304b–6a). Nevertheless, there is a clear and simple relationship between the heroic ethic when it is working well and that ethic when it has gone wrong. Beowulf states it:

> Ne sorga, snotor guma!   Selre bið æghwæm
> þæt he his freond wrece   þonne he fela murne.
> Ure æghwylc sceal   ende gebidan
> worolde lifes,   wyrce se þe mote
> domes ær deaþe;   þæt bið drihtguman
> unlifgendum   æfter selest.

> (1384–89)

Sooner or later all men die; Beowulf is saying. Let him who may get glory while he lives: that is best. And let those who are robbed of earthly felicity—cut off, like Aeschere—be avenged by their friends. The bargain may be bad, but the system appears still workable. Vengeance is compensation for a man's loss of earthly pleasure, that is, loss of Fulgentius' *primus*. Consider: Beowulf claimed in his flyting with Unferth, "Wyrd oft nereð / unfægne eorl, þonne his ellen deah" (572b–73). We are now in a position to understand this more fully.

Fate *may* cut a man down, as Aeschere was cut down by one of the "geosceaftgasta" (1266a), that is "fate-sent devils," and in this case vengeance must substitute for glory; but if a man keeps his wits about him and thus keeps his courage—and if fate happens not to be against him—he may come to happiness. Witness Beowulf's fight with Grendel as reported in the poet's summary statement in the second movement:

> þær him aglæca ætgræpe wearð;
> hwæþre he [Beowulf] gemunde mægenes strenge,
> gimfæste gife, ðe him God sealde,
> ond him to Anwaldan are gelyfde,
> frofre ond fultum; ðy he þone feond ofercwom,
> gehnægde helle gast.
>
> (1269–74a)

The events in the second movement dramatically elaborate these ideas.

Whatever earthly enjoyment Aeschere or Grendel might in later days have gotten from their deeds was nullified the moment they fell "fated." The Grendel's dam—Beowulf episode concerns, then, the second-best alternative, the pursuit of vengeance, on either side, which can result in payment for the murder and glory, either true or false, for the avenger. Throughout the episode, the poet focuses both by literal and by symbolic means on the way in which glory is kept or lost. This point needs no laboring. At the brink of Grendel's Mere, Unferth, still the foil (though recently some scholars are inclined to deny this), gives Beowulf his sword, frankly admitting that Beowulf is his better and showing his fear:

> . . . selfa ne dorste
> under yða gewin aldre geneþan,
> drihtscype dreogan; þær he dome forleas,
> ellenmærðum.
>
> (1468b–70b)

In the fight which Beowulf does have the valor and wisdom to undertake, the poet continually emphasizes the way Beowulf keeps his wits, his valor, and his awareness of the value of true fame, the lawful man's form of glory. References to these three elements, the equivalents of *arma, virum,* and *primus,* abound in lines 1473–1650. One example: "Eft waes anræd [resolute], nalas elnes [valor], / mærða [fame] gemyndig mæg Hyglaces . . ." (1529–30). The symbolic contrast to Beowulf is the sword Hrunting. Whereas Beowulf proves true, the sword proves inadequate: "seo ecg geswac / ðeodne æt þearfe" (1524–25a). Like Unferth, the sword "his dom alæg." Like Unferth, the sword has well-known virtues but is not up to the task set for it this time. The giant's sword Beowulf finds—a weapon as superior to Hrunting as Beowulf is to Unferth—is also symbolic. It is emblematic of the support given to human discernment by "witig God." Beowulf says:

> ac me geuðe   ylda Waldend,
> þæt ic on wage geseah   wlitig hangian
> ealdsweord eacen   —oftost wisode
> winigea leasum—,   þæt ic ðy wæpne gebræd.
>
> (1661–64)

Hrothgar's praise of Beowulf, back at Hart, is yet another restatement of the Fulgentian scheme (1700–1709a). Scops will say that all Beowulf's power (*arma*) he governed steadily by wisdom (*virum*), and therefore Hrothgar will again give Beowulf gifts which glorify him (*primus*). Hrothgar's "sermon" or speech of parting advice is, of course, his most important gift to Beowulf—a glorification which goes beyond the merely physical.

In his story of Heremod's perversion, and in the general conclusions he draws from this concerning pride and covetousness (1724b–52), Beowulf's instructor further elaborates the principle of Fulgentius' *primus* and hints at more than he knows about lasting glory. In language which at first glance seems strange for a pagan, he says to Beowulf, "Choose the better—eternal favor (*ece rædas*)." What he says next sounds equally Christian:

> Nu is þines mægnes blæd
> ane hwile;   eft sona bið,
> þæt ec adl oððe ecg   eafoþes getwæfeð,
> oððe fyres feng,   oððe flodes wylm,
> oððe gripe meces,   oððe gares fliht,
> oððe atol yldo;   oððe eagena bearhtm
> forsiteð ond forsworceð; semninga bið,
> þæt ðec, dryhtguma,   deað oferswyðeð.
>
> (1761–68)

However Christian these lines may sound, they express a pagan sentiment, though one which looks forward to a Christian idea. Since power declines, choose wisdom; avoid the pride and covetousness of Heremod.

In a pagan's mouth, the phrase *ece rædas* means, then, the lasting favor which comes from goodness. We have heard the phrase before. When Hama stole the necklace of the Brosings, he took it to his home city, *geceas ecne ræd*. The consistent Fulgentian scheme in the poem suggests that here the poet means not that Hama died (the usual interpretation) but that, as a treasure-getter like Scyld and the rest, he got the lasting favor of men who told his story. (The Hama digression occurs when Beowulf is being given gifts for his work and is thus glorified.) The pagan goal, fame, adumbrates a higher goal. Consider: Hrothgar, too, won glory by winning and dispensing treasures; but as he explicitly says in the lines immediately following those on mutability (just quoted), his experience with Grendel has shown him how little worldly glory (like Hama's) is worth. It is God he must thank for the cleansing of the hall. The eternal favor to be chosen, then, is not that of men but the favor of God, which one wins (as both the words and works of Beowulf have made Hrothgar see clearly) by courage and the discernment based on trust in wise God's judgment, and which one keeps by wise generosity, according to the code. He does *not* say "Choose heaven" but only "Choose continuing favor." In short, as he warns Beowulf about pride like Heremod's and urges him to seek God's favor, not man's, Hrothgar is preparing Beowulf for his old age.

The third movement further develops and closes the argument.

The Third Movement: Beowulf and Doom

The trouble with vengeance as compensation for the loss of felicity is tragically shown in Hrethel's house. One of Hrethel's sons kills the other by accident, and in such a case no avenging of the slain man is thinkable. Even the wisdom of Hrothgar would fail here. God's favor may send some comfort to a king in need of a champion, but no champion known to pagans can raise the dead or turn back the sorrow borne in mutability itself. This is the significance of Beowulf's successive confrontations with monsters. God in his wisdom can enable a shrewd and valiant hero to overcome the enemy of rational order, Grendel. And the God who won the war with the giants can enable a man to overcome perverse Power, the perverted irascibility of Grendel's dam, whose loyalty is not to Law but to an outlaw. But the prerevelation god of Hrothgar and Hygelac cannot overcome mutability itself, the destructive principle inherent in matter, slave to Fate—the principle traditionally represented in the figure of the dragon.[48]

The world of Beowulf is doomed. Men die, nations die, eventually the world itself will die. Hrothgar, in his speech on pride, gives part of the reason: *se weard swefeð*. This happens to individuals—Heremod, for instance—and perhaps even to nations. Consider the implications of Wealtheow's remarks to Beowulf on the harmony prevailing at Hart:

> "Her is æghwylc eorl   oþrum getrywe,
> modes milde,   mandrihtne hol[d],
> þegnas syndon geþwære,   þeod ealgearo,
> druncne dryhtguman   doð swa ic bidde!"
>
> (1228-31)

She is of course wrong, and when one recalls Hrothgar's words on the danger in too much success (1735 sq.), one sees in her touch of overconfidence an ominous sign.[49]

Nevertheless, insofar as the napping of intellect is the cause of disaster, men can take precautions. Some of these have been spelled out in the first two movements; one is developed almost entirely in the third. The first hint of this last came when Beowulf gave back Hrunting to Unferth, its owner:

> . . . sægde him þæs leanes þanc,
> cwæð, he þone guðwine   godne tealde,
> wigcræftigne,   nales wordum log
> meces ecge;   þæt wæs modig secg.
>
> (1809-12)

Donaldson wisely translates the last phrase, "he was a thoughtful man." In the dangerous Germanic world where hostility swells on mead to destruction, the highest discretion is not mere square dealing but generosity, charity, the ability to shrug off grudges. Beowulf is the model of this, a perfect thane. All his material gifts from Hrothgar he gives to Hygelac, and the poet comments:

> Swa sceal mæg don,
> nealles inwitnet   laþrum bregdon
> dyrnum cræfte,   deað ren(ian)
> hondgesteallan.   Hygelace wæs
> niða heardum   nefa swyðe hold,
> ond gehwæðer oðrum   hroþra gemyndig.
>
> (2166-71)

The poet adds a moment later that Beowulf

> dreah æfter dome;   nealles druncne slog
> heorðgeneatas;   næs him hreoh sefa,
> ac he mancynnes   mæste cræfte
> ginfæstan gife,   þe him God sealde,
> heold hildedeor.

(2179-83a)

It is in the poem's third movement that the significance of queens becomes explicit. They are the peace weavers—love is raised to national strategy. Hygd, Hygelac's queen, is called wise because she is generous to the Geats. She was once "mod þryth," an arrogant misuser of love (in her youth) but later became a woman famous for generosity and for her noble love of Offa.[50] It is through Ingeld's love for Hrothgar's daughter Freawaru that Hrothgar hopes to win peace between the Danes and the Heatho-Bards. But as Hildeburh's story has shown already, not even love—that is, not human love—is sufficient to turn away disaster. For all Freawaru can do, Beowulf predicts, some old Heatho-Bard will tempt some young one, through love of the young man's father and also through the young man's desire for the sword that ought to be his own, and war will break out again. Ingeld's "wife-love" will cool. (Cf. 2020-69.)

And so Hrothgar's account—*se weard swefeð*—is not the whole explanation. At least insofar as they care about the world, human beings are doomed at last—as doomed as was young Hondiscioh, swallowed by Grendel before he could lift a finger. The point is made by various dramatic means: the accidental murder of Hrethel's son; Hrothgar's sorrow when he parts with Beowulf, believing they will never meet again (1870 sq.); the sorrow Hygelac tells of feeling when Beowulf left him, going to almost certain death (1987 sq.). In none of these cases can anything be done. Wise or foolish, courageous or cowardly, man is the slave of Fate—or the slave of Fate at least until he abandons all things earthly for an other-worldly glory which, in Beowulf's time, is not yet available.[51] Thus, fittingly, the man who broke into the dragon's lair was some servant or slave who had no choice, who acted "nealles mid gewealdum . . . sylfes willum" (2221a-22a). And thus, fittingly, the dragon's hoard is the legacy of a dead race. Before the Incarnation, no final felicity or glory is visible to ordinary man, no *primus* like that with which Virgil left Aeneas. There is only fame like that of Hama, the "heroic" thief, or, at best, the fame of Beowulf who, though powerful, was gentle.

The story of the dragon robber grimly parodies all that has gone before. As Hrothgar and Beowulf won treasure, gave it out to others, and earned great glory, the paltry thief slips away with a cup, gives it to his angry master, and wins back his shelter. As both Beowulf and Grendel's dam sought vengeance, so the dragon—stupid, grotesque, terrible—hunts in anguish for its beloved cup and swears it will be avenged. The dragon strikes, destroys Beowulf's splendid hall; and Beowulf, in righteous indignation, strikes back.

His final battle is shot through with ambiguity, and both those critics who praise him for his final action and those who condemn him as overweening give us oversimplifications. It is true that once again, apparently, Beowulf refuses all counsel, but it is not at all clear that the counsel he gets is wise (see 3077–83). It is true that Beowulf's mistake—if it *is* one—coupled with the lack of valor in all but one of his retainers, brings on the end of the Geatish nation; or at any rate, Wiglaf predicts this result, and the poet says Wiglaf is largely right (2864–3030a). And it is true, moreover, that the end of the poem has a kind of ghastly irony. Beowulf thinks he has done a great deed, thinks he has won a splendid treasure which will give honor and power to his people; but in fact the gold he won lies in the ground "eldum swa unnyt   swa hi[t aero]r wæs" (3168).[52] And so, from one point of view, Beowulf's death is—in a strictly modern sense—absurd. Still, gold or no gold, he has saved the nation from an intolerable evil, the dragon. With his fall, the Geatish nation falls; but would the nation have flourished—would it even have survived—had Beowulf declined the fight? The poet's suggestion is that the tribe was doomed in any case by its own earlier violence and greed. The killing of the dragon is closely identified (by rhythmic encoding of the Caedmonic type) with Hygelac's murder of old King Ongentheow by Wulf and Eofor (*greed* and *ill-will*), sons of Wanred (dark-counsel). Beowulf, like all men, is guilty by association.

The *Beowulf*-poet's concern with the themes *valor, wisdom,* and *glory* may or may not reflect the influence of Fulgentius' reading of the *Aeneid*. It would be foolish to look for precise parallels between the English poem and Fulgentius' *Expositio,* since we know before we start that Beowulf has no Dido, no Cerberus, no Caieta. More important, as I have said, the *Beowulf*-poet focuses on decline and old age (first Hrothgar, then Beowulf), matters outside the scope of Virgil's poem. But since the *Aeneid* is frequently cited as a likely influence on *Beowulf,* and since the *Aeneid,* in the English poet's time, was normally read in Fulgentius' way, as a poem using what I have called "vertical allegory," a few general parallels between *Beowulf* and the *Aeneid* as read by Fulgentius may be worth mentioning. Allusion and imitation, after all, are obvious ways of allegorically charging an image or event.

For Fulgentius, water in the *Aeneid* everywhere signifies either birth (Juno's storm) or the troubles of youth. It seems possible to consider the deeds of Beowulf before the action of the poem—the swim with Breca, the fights with water monsters, etc.—as the first Fulgentian phase. (Beowulf himself refers to these as accomplishments of his youth.) This is not at all to deny that on another level water may work as Nicholson thinks, as that which separates heaven and earth. The storm and monsters may be directly equivalent to Fulgentius' powers of Aeolus (Perdition), since obviously they are evil—symbols of the evil which is slain in baptism, Nicholson argues[53]—and since the feast they look forward to is analogous to Grendel's demonic feasting and antitypic of the Christian celestial banquet. For Aeneas' Cyclops ("ignorance and quarrelsomeness") Beowulf has Unferth, who is certainly ignorant of what really happened in the swimming match. But these allusive possibilities must be taken as strictly tentative. If the Woden-priest Unferth (one-eyed in St. Augustine's sense) is at first analogous to the Cyclops, he becomes, later, a generous but cowardly, very human thane. Hygd changes still more drastically. The poet's mixture of ethical traits in his characters is a reason not to take any character as consistently symbolic by Fulgentius' standards.

But other allegorical standards do apply. As we have said, no biblical exegete demands exact conjunctions of Old and New Testament events. *Beowulf* is clearly a work in which the pagan intuition of Hrothgar and Beowulf anticipates revelation. It is just as clearly, on one level, a celebration of the best possible human—perhaps divinely inspired—code. Christianity wins by default on this level, and the points at which the life of Beowulf calls to mind the life of Christ can be understood as signals of the level's central irony. If, in terms of the ethic of noble service, wisdom, and reward, Beowulf seems cheated in his old age (his joy as he dies is partly delusion), so all good men must appear to be cheated prior to man's knowledge of Christ, who can raise the dead and pay them as they deserve. (The poet, however, knows the truth about virtuous pagans: "him of hræðre gewat / sawol secean soðfæstra dom," [2819b–20].) The hero is unquestionably "Christlike": as Beowulf alone overcame the demonic enemy of all (699), Christ overcame the devil; as Beowulf's mother might well say that "the God of Old was kind to her in her childbearing" (942b sq.), so the Virgin might say; as Beowulf's men give up all hope in the ninth hour (1600a), so did the disciples at the crucifixion; and as Beowulf was survived by twelve, so was Christ. Of each of them, Christ and Beowulf, it may be said that he was

> wyruldcyning[a],
> manna mildust   ond mon (ðw)ærust,
> leodum liðost,   lofgeornost
>
> (3180–82)

—if we take *lofgeornost* to mean eager for "glory" in the higher sense toward which Hrothgar's last speech to Beowulf points us. One may of course go much further. In his first great battle, Beowulf killed nine sea monsters; Christ in his first great battle expelled defectors from nine angelic legions. (Beowulf's banquet joke in his answer to Unferth is interesting, in this light. For the poet's audience, it alludes to Christ himself as banquet of the blessed.) The Grendel's Mere episode is parallel to Christ's crucifixion and harrowing of hell (the ninth hour; the stock associations of the burning lake; the search of the cave by the light of a sword hilt, which riddle writers might read as a cross, as in, apparently, Riddle #55). And the dragon episode may have to do, on its deepest level, with Armageddon and Last Judgment.[54]

Clearly the relationship between Christ and Beowulf can be seen as, at least on one level, ironic. The poem is full of cups, and the emphasis on this image can be explained by the importance of the eucharistic cup in Christian worship; but these cups are not eucharistic: they make men "beore druncne," so that a man like Beowulf who never gets drunk and slays kinsmen is worthy of remark. The poem is full of treasures, emblematic perhaps of the treasures of heaven; but these are not heavenly treasures: they are "hæðen gold" (2276b), laid up in the earth where rust corrupts and thieves break in and steal. The irony is dramatic: the Christ toward whom Beowulf's life and character point (like a "beacon") redeems what would have seemed, before revelation, the tragedy of Beowulf the good man.[55]

5

Elene and the
Dream of the Rood

Both Caedmonic poetry and that stylistic strain represented by
Beowulf, the *Wanderer,* and the *Seafarer,* use allegorizing devices,
Caedmonic poetry in a way that simultaneously underlines the
harmony of scripture and adapts it to Germanic culture, the second
strain in a way that gives Christian interpretation to pagan or secular
material. The Caedmonic strain brings scripture to Germania; the
Beowulfian brings Germania to church. The poetry of Cynewulf,
probably influenced by both Caedmonic and Beowulfian methods,
marks a breakthrough in stylistic evolution: Cynewulf makes moral
allegory of saints' lives, meditations, and the like. (The same method
was an Irish commonplace.) Whereas the *Beowulf*-poet finds Christian
tropological content in the life of a pagan hero, Cynewulf reads the
life of a saint in eschatological terms. Whereas the *Physiologus*-poet
and the *Phoenix*-poet (the latter conceivably Cynewulf himself) find
moral lessons through an allegorical view of creatures, Cynewulf
finds moral instruction in the experience of the cross. Like Caedmonic
poetry, the poetry of Cynewulf assumes a direct analogy of pagan experience and Christian, and explores each in terms of the other.
Rightly understood, Cynewulfian style is not a sorry decline from
classical Old English poetic style (except in terms of meter) but a
change, a shift in emphasis—in rhetorical terms, a shift from the
Ciceronian and Augustinian rhetoric of logic and rational persuasion
to a Christianized sophistic rhetoric of intricacy and decoration. The

latter is, technically, decadent. But there is much to be said for the intellectual games of weary sophisticates. When a man has looked for a hundred years at a statue of a discus thrower, he begins to think, "So what?"

Elene

The specific text or group of texts which Cynewulf used in composing *Elene* cannot be identified among the texts which have survived, but it is clear that with respect to plot, the English poet must have followed closely the tradition available to him.[1] Having before us Holthausen's collations of *Elene* with other versions of the cross legend,[2] we are in a position to examine Cynewulf's contribution in detail. We have also Claes Schaar's very general discussion of Cynewulf's use of his sources. The chief difference, an important one, is that—as Schaar conservatively puts it, "the style of Cynewulf's poem is much fuller than that in the Latin legends."[3] Some details of plot are peculiar to *Elene*. One is the episode concerning the message to Constantine after the finding of the cross, the joy of the emperor and his subjects, and the emperor's return message to Elene ordering her to build a church (967–1016). Other details peculiar to this poem are the elaborate description of the approach of the enemies of Rome, the battle, and the victory of Constantine (18b–53, 105–43); Elene's voyage to the land of the Jews (225–75); and, of course, the presumably autobiographical close of the poem (1236–1321). Among details commonly found in the tradition but missing from *Elene* are the queen's interest in the tradition about the crucifixion and her destruction of the temple of Venus.[4]

If we assume a lost source containing all relevant elements of the Latin texts which have been identified as close to *Elene*—notably the Vita Quiriaci of the *Acta Sanctorum*,[5] the *Inventio Sanctae Crucis*,[6] and the legend in the *Vitae Sanctorum*[7]—we may reasonably suppose that Cynewulf's embellishment of the traditional plot is little more than dutiful *amplificatio* of the sort already accepted by the Church as a means of drawing simple men to redemption.[8] But the assumption of a single source is by no means securely founded. As Dubois has shown,[9] Cynewulf's division of humanity into three groups, at the close of *Elene*, draws from the *Sermo* CIV, 8, of St. Augustine,[10] which contains the same division. Sarrazin and Schaar, among others, have convincingly argued extensive borrowing from *Beowulf* within the Elene story,[11] and have shown the same influence at work in other of the signed Cynewulfian poems. Without descending to less forceful evidence—such as Carleton Brown's note on correspondences between *Elene* and a Middle Irish version, the fourteenth-century *Leabhar Breac*,[12] or Professor Grau's parallels between *Elene* and a sermon by St. Ephrem the Syrian[13]—we can safely believe that Cynewulf's method was, as he tells us in his epilogue, a careful sorting and organizing of diverse materials "swa ic on bocum fand" (1254b), in other words, *inventio* of a high order.[14] The view that here Cynewulf manipulated diverse sources for an original purpose accords with what we know of his handling of sources elsewhere among the signed poems or in *Guthlac B*, which draws freely from Felix's *Vita S. Guthlaci* V,[15] from the *Carmen de Resurrectione Mortuorum*,[16] and from Anglo-Saxon elegiac tradition, possibly the *Wanderer*, as Kennedy suggests.[17] And the view that Cynewulf makes a free use of sources for some purpose of his own has the indirect support of his stylistic practice. His fondness for establishing structural parallels, ironic juxtapositions of scenes, and verbal repetition all indicate more than a pious recorder's interest in form.

These considerations invite us to examine *Elene* from within—bearing in mind the additions to and deletions from the traditional story, insofar as these can be determined. Stylistic analysis reveals that *Elene* is a poem consciously and thematically developed and that the epilogue is an integral part of the poet's statement. The poem is organized in terms of what the cross did with and for (1) Constantine, (2) Judas, and (3) the poet; and in each case a contrast is established between the idea of universal Christendom and the narrower Germanic ideal, clan loyalty. Thus Cynewulf's transfer of classical Old English devices to a new context is functional as well as ornamental, supporting the poet's central concern with a Germanic motif which the Anglo-Saxon audience, presumably familiar with Caedmonic technique, would readily grasp and appreciate.

The theme of the poem, explicitly presented in the epilogue, is the contrast between the universal Christian ethic and the so-called heroic ethic. This theme Cynewulf develops in two spheres—the temporal, represented by Constantine, and the ecclesiastical, represented by Judas Cyriacus—and on three levels, as a conflict between Satan and God, as a conflict between hostile clans here on earth, and finally as a conflict with the individual human heart, that of the poet. The unifying image, important not only to action but also to symbolic structure, is the cross; a secondary related image is fire.

From a technical standpoint, the principle of organization is, with one striking difference, the principle of exemplum and analysis which informs the *Physiologus,* the *Phoenix,* the *Wanderer,* the *Seafarer,* and other Old English Christian works. The Constantine-Elene-Judas story is treated as exemplary or "typical" and is analyzed in the epilogue for its allegorical content. In other words, just as the Seafarer's experience is first presented virtually without comment, then, in effect, analyzed for its moral signification, so the traditional Elene story is presented dramatically, then moralized in the epilogue. The striking difference—which *Elene* shares with the *Dream of the Rood*—is that the allegorical analysis is for the most part not explicit but implied. The connections between the story and the epilogue are clearly indicated, however, and are neatly schematic. For the poet, Elene's relationship to Constantine is analogous to Christ's relationship to God; her relationship to Judas is analogous to Christ's redeeming and judgmental relationship to the individual sinner; and Judas's loyalty to the narrow clan, as opposed to universal Christendom, is analogous to the individual's mistaken loyalty to the flesh, in other words, man's concupiscence. Cynewulf's known or probable departures from the traditional plot can in every case be explained by his concern with maintaining the consistency of the exemplum. Two examples may be mentioned at once. The traditional account of the queen's inquiries into the story of the crucifixion is deleted (supposing Cynewulf knew this detail) first because in this poem the queen's authority—not identical with God's but metaphorically parallel to God's—cannot be so drastically undercut, and, second, because the detail cannot possibly admit of allegorical analysis in the epilogue. Her destruction of the temple of Venus is deleted from Cynewulf's version because it would interfere with the simple opposition of king and usurper, God and Satan: Satan, not Venus, usurps the loyalty of the Jews, in Cynewulf's version.

The preparation for battle, which opens the poem, is almost completely Cynewulf's work. He takes from his source the basic elements of the dramatic situation—the numerical advantage of the opposition, the river separating the two armies, and a comment that Constantine is fearful.[18] He adds what has sometimes been described (not unjustly) as "conventional imitation of heroic Old English verse." The passage is defensible in terms of theme. Before his vision, Constantine is in effect a tribal chieftain concerned with preserving his people from hostile bands. He and his comitatus know and live by the heroic ethic, which preserves men from shame but cannot preserve them from death, as all the imagery insists and as the epilogue will state (in the opening lines of the "signature"). In the parallel passages dealing with the enemy's mustering of troops (18b–41a) and the Roman mustering of troops (41a–68), Cynewulf focuses on the seeming hopelessness of the Roman cause. The enemy gathers confidently and openly, as bold and swift and noisy as the animals with which this host is associated, the wolf and the eagle:

> Fyrdleoð agol
> wulf on wealde,   wælrune ne mað.
> Urigfeðera   earn sang ahof,
> laðum on laste.
>
>   (27b–30a)

They march to the Danube and there, when night falls, stand roaring with confidence, expecting to destroy the Roman tribe.

> Werodes breahtme
> woldon Romwara   rice geþringan,
> hergum ahyðan.
>
>   (39b–41a)

The Romans, on the other hand, gather in frightened confusion—hornbearers leaping, messengers shouting. The animal associated with their army is the raven.[19] Constantine's fear, probably suggested by a single word, *timuit,* in Cynewulf's source, is developed through thirteen lines (56b–68), capped by a conventional Germanic image which enforces the contrast between the two armies. Across the Danube from the roaring enemy, the Romans sleep "eorlas ymb æþeling."

Then comes, as in the sources, the vision of the cross, emblem of a system that can save men from death itself and standard of a kingdom far greater than Constantine's. The king carries the cross into battle, and, to the music of ravens, God's retainers rout the enemy. The raising of the cross (123b sq.) marks a turning point not only in the battle but in the poet's treatment of images as well. Images of darkness and turbulent motion come to be applied to the enemy; images of light and song are applied to the Romans (even the wolf and eagle are forgotten). To this contrast of images the poet will repeatedly return. The opening of the poem sets up, both dramatically and imagistically, the theme and pattern of the whole.

Back in Rome Constantine learns (as in the sources) the meaning of the sign. It represents the King of Heaven, a point Cynewulf underscores by variation and verbal repetition: "heofoncyninges [tacen]," "se gasta helm," and "cyninga wuldor"; the sign is a defense against

hostile kingdoms—"wið þeoda þræce." The Roman king accepts baptism and becomes (reading literally) both king and retainer to a higher
king: "goldwine gumena in godes þeowdom" (201).

Through study of the scriptures, Constantine learns (as in Cynewulf's source) of the murder of Christ. Cynewulf alone, however,
treats Satan's seduction of the Jews as a trick played by a usurper
king on a tumultuous crowd (205–10a). Constantine sends Elene to
deal with *Iudea cyn* and recover the cross.

The lines devoted to the journey of Elene and her army—original
with Cynewulf—serve a number of functions. First, verbal echoes and
imagistic parallels recall the earlier passage on the movement of the
enemies of Rome toward the Danube: like Rome's enemies, the queen's
army hurries to the rim of a surging waterway and there—Cynewulf
mentions this detail twice—the queen's army pauses, as did the enemy
of Rome on reaching the Danube. The structural echo calls attention
to the change in the Roman's situation: fighting for God, they are
now on the winning side, the position Rome's enemies seemed to
occupy in the earlier passage. Second, and more important, by inserting the passage on Elene's journey, Cynewulf is able to emphasize the
loyalty of Elene and her forces, in contrast to the disloyalty of the
Jewish clan, which the poet mentioned immediately above. Constantine tells his mother to seek eagerly—"georne secan" (216b)—and
the eagerness with which she and her band obey their lord is the focus
of the whole Cynewulfian insertion. Concerning Elene, the poet says:

> Elene ne wolde
> þæs siðfates   sæne weorðan,
> ne ðæs wilgifan   word gehyrwan,
> hiere sylfre suna,   ac wæs sona gearu
> wif on willsið,   swa hire weoruda helm,
> byrnwiggendra,   beboden hæfde.
>
> (219b–24)

They pause only for a moment before the fiercely surging billows,
then press on, and the focus of the imagery remains on the churning,
pounding, and roaring of the sea, the terrors which imply the valor of
the undaunted invasion force. The passage reads:

> Þær wlanc manig   æt Wendelsæ
> on stæðe stodon.   Stundum wræcon
> ofer mearopaðu   mægen æfter oðrum,

ond þa gehlodon   hildesercum,
bordum ond ordum,   byrnwigendum,
werum ond wifum,   wæghengestas.
Leton þa ofer fifelwæg   famige scriðan
bronte brimþisan.   Bord oft onfeng
ofer earhgeblond   yða swengas;
sæ swinsade.   Ne hyrde ic sið ne ær
on egstreame   idese lædan,
on merestræte,   maegen fægerre.
Þær meahte gesion,   se ðone sið beheold,
brecan ofer bæðweg,   brimwudu snyrgan
under swellingum,   sæmearh plegean,
wadan wægflotan.

                                        (231–46a)

It is generally agreed that the direct source of Cynewulf's treatment
of the army's boarding and launching is *Beowulf*, lines 207b–18 (in
Klaeber's text).[20] The source differs chiefly from Cynewulf's imitation
in that there is less noise and violent motion, or, to put it abusively,
less hysteria in the *Beowulf*:

                              fiftyna sum
sundwudu sohte;   secg wisade,
lagucræftig mon   landgemyrcu.
Fyrst forð gewat;   flota wæs on yðum,
bat under beorge.   Beornas gearwe
on stefn stigon—   streamas wundon,
sund wið sande;   secgas bæron
on bearm nacan   beorhte frætwe,
guðsearo geatolic;   guman ut scufon,
weras on wilsið   wudu bundenne.
Gewat þa ofer wægholm   winde gefysed
flota famiheals   fugle gelicost. . . .

                                        (*Beowulf*, 207b–18)

The lines cry out for Wagnerian French horns, and to compare them
with the breathless bassoons of Cynewulf is inhumane. Nevertheless,
Cynewulf's histrionic intensification of the imagery, his insistence on
the dramatically irrelevant difficulty of the voyage, is thematically
sound. Here as so often in Cynewulf, we are dealing with picture-
window emblems, not realistic pictures.

Difficult as their voyage is, Elene and her army are serene. The
reason is presented imagistically: their whole band gleams with gold
and gems given to them by their lord, Constantine, to whom they have

been, and are yet, so loyal. The gems recall the gems with which the victors' shields were adorned and look forward to the gems which will adorn the rediscovered cross—gems emblematic of heavenly reward. Thus the Cynewulfian insertion emphasizes the cosmic loyalty theme and comments on the disloyalty of the nation Elene comes to chastize.

Elene's successive confrontations of the Jewish wise men—three thousand, then one thousand, then five hundred, and finally Judas alone—are found in the sources. Throughout this section of the poem, Cynewulf follows his source very closely. His changes are significant but minor, and I will not dwell on them. He consistently changes *dei* to *King* or some extended periphrastic designation meaning king and identifying the Jews as God's former retainers. For instance, they were once loved by "wuldorcyninge" and were "dryhtne dyre," (291b, 292a) both probably translating a single phrase, "dilecti dei."[21] The Jewish wise men are characterized more fully and viewed more sympathetically than in the nearest surviving source, where they are simply "legis doctores."[22] And Judas's role is expanded.

In Cynewulf's poem, the confrontations give dignity to the Jews, who are rather elaborately characterized as men of great wisdom who are guilty only through the sins of their fathers (as in the sources) since they themselves—all but Judas—are ignorant of the crime. The confrontations also give dignity to Elene, who is characterized as at once intransigent and merciful, like Christ himself, firm in resolution but also eager to win the Jews to repentance. Her inquiry about the crucifixion, as I have said, is suppressed.

In the first confrontation, here as in the sources, she castigates the Jews for the murder of Christ; but learning that they do not know what she means, she explains more fully in the second confrontation, first reminding them of their former virtue—in Cynewulf's version, the former nobility of their kingdom—and recalling to them the words of their prophets. She rebukes them for having followed error and charges them to find wise men who can give information, as Cynewulf has it, "out of their deep minds." When she confronts the five hundred, the queen again appeals to the Jews' loyalty to their own tradition and tribe—a detail inserted here by Cynewulf. The Jews, knowing nothing of the long-hidden crime, answer in the only way they can; and when the queen sends them out to try once more, the poet says sympathetically, once more introducing materials of his own,

Eodon þa fram rune,   swa him sio rice cwen,
  bald in burgum,   beboden hæfde,

geomormode,　　georne smeadon,
sohton searoþancum,　　hwæt sio syn wære
þe hie on þam folce　　gefremed hæfdon
wið pam casere,　　þe him sio cwen wite.

(411–16)

The narrowing of the field of wise men leads at last to Judas, the dramatically central character in the poem.

The reason Judas does not want to reveal the secret which only he knows is that he is committed to and limited by heroic code: to confess to the murder of Christ would be to destroy the Jewish tribe, he says. Judas and Constantine, it should be noticed, have the same commitment initially, loyalty to the clan; but whereas this loyalty leads Constantine to accept the cross and transfer his loyalty to God, who will preserve the Romans, the same loyalty in a different situation leads Judas to deny the cross.

The poet focuses sharply on Judas's anguish, expanding his source to dramatize Judas's grief and shame over the sin of the Jews.[23] But despite his grief and shame, Judas tells his fellow counsellors,

Nu is þearf mycel
þæt we fæstlice　　ferhð staðelien,
þæt we ðæs morðres　　meldan ne weorðen
hwær þæt halige trio　　behelded wurde
æfter wigþræce,　　þy læs toworpen sien
frod fyrngewritu　　ond þa fæderlican
lare forleten.　　Ne bið lang ofer ðæt
þæt Israhela　　æðelu moten
ofer middangeard　　ma ricsian
æcræft eorla,　　gif ðis yppe bið

(426–35)

When Elene is at last provoked to a threat (original with Cynewulf) that she will burn and kill them, the wise men deliver up Judas (as in the sources), throwing the burden of decision on him. Elene gives Judas the choice of life or death, and Judas answers hopelessly but bravely with a grim parody of one of Christ's sayings (a detail Cynewulf found in his source). After his bitter joke, he says he will die for his loyalty. But he cannot, he finds. Here as elsewhere in hagiographic literature, including Cynewulf's sources, Christianity first wins by force, that same awesome power by which Constantine overcame his enemies early in the poem. Conversion and revelation come later. Half-starved, in the pit where Elene has thrown him, and too weak to pursue his stubborn will, Judas capitulates.

From here to the conclusion of the Elene story, Cynewulf follows his source very closely, deviating only to emphasize significant parallels, images, and ideas. His original passage of the triumphant return of the messengers to Rome, the joy of the emperor and his people and the emperor's command that a splendidly adorned church be built recall the earlier voyage of Elene and her host, the earlier joy in military victory, and the earlier adorning of the victors' shields with jewels. (This time it is the cross that is adorned with jewels.) All these details are Cynewulf's invention. The emperor's joy is parallel to the queen's joy in the conversion and intensified intellectual power of Judas, after his flyting with the devil. (The queen's joy at this point is also Cynewulf's invention.) In both cases, the joy dramatizes another contrast between the heroic ethic and the Christian. The crime of the Jewish tribe has been established by Cynewulf as the murder of a king, and in terms of the heroic ethic, the payment for that is what Judas wrongly predicted it would be if ever the cross were found: death for the betrayers. But the King of Heaven does not demand blood payment: he prefers correction of old error, renunciation of the false king who misled the people, Satan. God's object is Kingdom Come, the supremacy of Christendom not only in heaven but also here on earth.

Within the poem, as parallels invented by Cynewulf make clear, God achieves this object through the power of the cross. Won over by the military puissance of the cross (as in the sources), Constantine fights and puts to rout the temporal enemies of God; won over by the spiritual power of the cross (as in the sources) Judas fights and puts to flight the false king himself, Satan. Cynewulf develops this balance further. By the temporal authority of Constantine and through the ecclesiastical authority of Judas, and again through the agency of Elene, in Cynewulf's version, Constantine receives the bridle which helps to make him an invincible defender of Christendom. At Jerusalem the true cross works spiritual miracles; at Rome the nails give might in battle. Both Constantine and Judas are vassals of God, and Elene, as servant of the Roman king and intermediary between him and her temporary spiritual lord, Judas Cyriacus, is in Cynewulf's version the vassal and agent of both. The diagram of feudal relationships thus established from the King of Heaven downward—not to be found in the sources—is itself a cross:

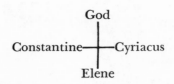

The symbol of Christ's overpowering of death becomes the scheme of Christendom.

The parallels between the Elene story and the poet's own spiritual story are worked out in the epilogue. To Constantine, Judas, and Elene, and then to the poet, the cross gives wisdom and power. Through the power of the cross, Constantine wins the victory which opens the poem, and after the king has learned of Christ and accepted him, the emperor becomes wise in scripture (198–202). When Judas meets the devil, the Holy Ghost kindles within him such prophetic wisdom and might that he can overthrow the usurper. Elene is astonished at Judas's new wisdom (952–61). Elene, too, though only incidentally, wins power and wisdom. After the finding of the nails, the poet says of her,

> Heo gefylled wæs
> wisdomes gife,   ond þa wic beheold
> halig heofonlic gast,   hreðer weardode,
> aeðelne innoð;   swa hie ælmihtig
> sigebearn godes   sioððan freoðode.

                                            (1142b–46)

(This detail is in the sources.) In similar fashion, study of the cross legend brings "wisdom" to the poet, and it also brings a kind of power, the art of poetry by which at long last he "reveals" the story of the cross. Cynewulf writes:

> Þus ic frod onf fus   þurh þæt fæcne hus
> wordcræftum wæf   ond wundrum læs,
> þragum þreodude   ond geþanc reodode
> nihtes nearwe.   Nysse ic gearwe
> be ðere rode riht   ær me rumran geþeaht
> þurh ða mæran miht   on modes þeaht
> wisdom onwreah.   Ic wæs weorcum fah,
> synnum asælde,   sorgum gewæled,
> bitrum gebunded,   bisgum beþrungen,
> ær me lare onlag   þurh leohtne had
> gamelum to geoce,   gife unscynde

mægencyning amæt   ond on gemynd begeat,
torht ontynde,   tidum gerymde,
bancofan onband,   breostlocan onwand,
leoðucræft onleac.

(1236–50a)

The poet's experience is closely parallel to the experience of Judas. Whereas Judas lay in a pit close to death, the poet was "fus" in the sense of "near death" and imprisoned—so to speak—in "fæcne hus" and "nihtes nearwe." He was, as he says, shackled in sin, enclosed by trouble, and, like Judas, stained by old evil. Just as Judas finds that the lesser must give way to the greater—the weaker human being to the stronger and the separate clan to the Kingdom of God—so the poet in his anguish learns a wider vision than he formerly possessed and, at *last* (as he says) reveals it. The cross—he means here the legend of the cross—is a kind of riddle which Cynewulf has been allowed to solve. He says:

Ic þæs wuldres treowes
oft, nales æne,   hæfde ingemynd
ymb þone beorhtan beam . . .

(1251b–54a)

The solution appears in the famous lines containing the poet's signature.

A wæs secg oð ðæt
cnyssed cearwelmum,   ᚻ drusende   (cene)
þeah he in medohealle   maðmas þege,
æplede gold.   ᚠ gnornode   (yr)[24]
ᚦ gefera,   nearusorge dreah,   (nyd)
enge rune,   þær him ᛗ fore   (eoh)
milpaðas meat,   modig þrægde
wirum gewlenced.   ᚹ is geswiðrad,   (wyn)
gomen æfter gearum,   geogoð is gecyrred,
ald onmedla.   ᚢ wæs geara   (ur)
geogoðhades blæm.   Nu synt geardagas
æfter fyrstmearce   forð gewitene,
lifwynne geliden,   swa ᛚ toglideð,   (lagu)
flodas gefysde.   ᚠ æghwam bið   (feoh)
læne under lyfte;   landes frætwe
gewitaþ under wolcnum   winde gelicost,
þonne he for hæleðum   huld astigeð,

wæðeð be wolcnum,   wedende færeð
ond eft semninga   swige gewyrðeð,
in nedcleofan   nearwe geheaðrod,
þream forþrycced.

(1256b–75a)

There was once the age of the youthful and proud hero who won appled gold and meadhall treasure but was doomed to die—beaten (like the Danube or like Elene's ships) by surging "waves," here waves of sorrow—in short, the age of the young clan; but that has given way to the age of decline and misery, here associated with man's old age and with the withering and imprisonment of earth in winter. A third age will follow, the age of the Last Judgement and Kingdom Come.

As Judas faced the intransigent Elene, who (only in Cynewulf's version) threatened fire and death (574–84), so every man must face the intransigent final Judge, who threatens ultimate fire and death. Just as Judas, misguided by pride—a virtue within the heroic ethic— spoke foolishly at first, so the poet and every man

　　　　　　　　riht gehyran
dæda gehwylcra   þurh þæs deman muð,
ond worda swa same   wed gesyllan,
eallra unsnyttro   ær gesprecenra,
þristra   geþonca.

(1282–86a)

But just as Elene desired the capitulation of her enemy, so Christ desires the heart's conversion; and as Elene elevated Judas Cyriacus, so Christ lifts the penitent sinner out of the two painful regions of the three-level fire.

This three-level fire is prepared by earlier imagery in the poem. The devil and his legion, whose sin is pride, live underground. For his pride, Judas is cast in a pit from which only his submission to God's in- strument can save him. The ascension of Christ from underground to heaven is repeatedly mentioned, as is the idea of man's escape from the grave to the abode of angels (e. g., in Judas's prayer; all significant elements of the prayer are found in the source, but in no extant source does the pattern extend to the rest of the work). The poet speaks often of how wrong it is that the cross should lie hidden underground, and once it is found it is covered with precious gems emblematic of heavenly treasure or victory.

The poet develops, then, a rough system of relationships based on the Germanic, as well as Christian, underworld, mid-world, upper-world concept: devils, men, angels; death, human life, eternal life; pride, Christian submission, wisdom and bliss; and the lowest, middle, and highest levels of the ultimate fire (1286b–1302a). On the moral level, this three-stage scheme corresponds to the movement in the life of man from the pride of youth to the suffering and doubt of age to salvation or damnation in the final judgment. On the level of history, the scheme corresponds to the progress from the heroic youth of the Germanic band (the age of the richly adorned horse) to the decline of the band, when "the adornments of earth vanish," to acceptance or rejection of universal Christendom.

The *Dream of the Rood*

Though the *Dream of the Rood* is not one of Cynewulf's signed poems, scholars are generally in agreement that the poem is his.[25] Subject matter, style, and sentiment all suggest the same hand that wrote the *Elene*. In both celebrations of the power of the cross, the heroic ethic and the Christian are systematically contrasted by means of phrases which enforce an ironic analogy; and both poems seem to be constructed by means of a skillful interweaving of diverse source materials. In the *Elene* the ironic analogy and the interweaving of source materials is clear: the length of the poem offers cumulative internal evidence, and we have for that poem sources which are close enough that we can with fair confidence study the poet's way of manipulating sources. In the case of the *Dream,* the whole matter of sources is more doubtful, and we must work primarily, though not exclusively, from internal evidence.

Bruce Dickins and Alan S. C. Ross, in their edition of the *Dream,* treat two possible sources, the texts inscribed on the famous Ruthwell and Brussels crosses, then treat more distant literary relationships, notably Riddles 31, 56, and 73.[26] They point out that the passages found on the Ruthwell Cross (the closest source) correspond to passages found in the first half of the Vercelli text, that "the last few lines, referring to the Harrowing of Hell, have all the appearance of an addition," and that "stylistically the poem seems to divide at 1.78."[27] The conclusion Dickins and Ross reach, that "the Vercelli Text is probably composite,"[28] is undoubtedly sound. It seems far more likely, in fact, that the poet weaved various older materials together in composing the *Dream* than that he used no specific sources but composed "from personal emotion," whatever that may mean, as the editors suggest later.[29] Both the harrowing of hell section of the *Dream* and the passages showing the influence of hymns from the Latin liturgy, such as the "Pange Lingua" and "Vexilla Regis" of Venantius Fortunatus,[30] would seem to argue composition by systematic application of the rhetorical principles of the poet's day. It should be added, however, that very little of the total poem can be accounted for through sources thus far identified. In both the Brussels and Ruthwell cross inscriptions, the cross speaks in the first person. The Brussels Cross speaks of carrying the powerful king, of trembling, and of being made wet with blood ("blode bestemed"), then tells who ordered this cross erected. The longer Ruthwell Cross inscription tells how God mounted the cross by choice ("he wolde on galgu gestiga"), perhaps gives an image also found in the *Dream*, "stained with blood" —but the reading is uncertain: only "odig f" remains of the hypothetical "blodig fah." It tells, like the cross in the *Dream*, of its own fear of bowing against the Lord's wish ("hylda ic ni dorste"), tells of men gathered near, speaks of being "wiþ blodse bestemed"—again the reading is uncertain—and has, in addition, the phrase found in the *Dream*, "Krist wæs on rodi," the image of coming from afar, the phrase "wounded with shafts" (*strelum giwundad*), and, finally, the image of Christ's wearied limbs. While these similarities are too close to be effects of chance, they tell us very little about the poet's method. The other identifiable sources—the Latin hymns, etc.—are equally distant, merely close enough to support a hypothesis that the poem was constructed out of various materials.

Whether or not interweaving like that in the *Elene* is one of the *Dream*-poet's central methods, it is clear that the poet uses pagan-Christian analogy like that in Caedmonic poetry, in *Beowulf*, and in *Elene*—a consistent comparison of pagan Germanic and Christian premises. The opposition was undoubtedly more obvious to the poet's original audience than it is to us, and for them it must surely have heightened the poem's aesthetic and devotional effect. In the *Dream of the Rood* three traditional Germanic themes are developed ironically and thus converted to Christian use: the theme of exile, of heroic loyalty, and the theme of reward.

We have seen already that the exile theme is expressed in many Anglo-Saxon poems—the *Wanderer*, the *Seafarer*, the *Wife's Lament*, *Beowulf*, and elsewhere. Let us look at the theme more closely now. The exile suffers from the hostility of the elements, from loneliness, and, above all, from the loss of his lord's love and protection. Thus the Wanderer says:

> Wyn eal gedreas!
> Forþon wat se þe sceal   his winedryhtnes
> leofes larcwidum   longe forþolian,
> ðonne sorg and slæp   somod ætgædre
> earmne anhogan   oft gebindað.
> þinceð him on mode   þæt he his mondryhten
> clyppe and cysse,   ond on cneo lecge
> honda ond heafod,   swa he whilum ær
> in geardagum   giefstolas breac.
> Donne onwæcneð eft   wineless guma,
> gesihð him biforan   fealwe wegas,
> baþian brimfuglas,   brædan feþra,
> hreosan hrim ond snaw,   hagle gemenged.

> _(Wanderer,_ 36b–48)

The solitary man's idea of happiness is return to the meadhall with all
its song and joy, and his bitterest expression of his present misery
takes the form of grim comparison of his lonely and comfortless
situation to his former meadhall pleasures. The Seafarer relates how,
sailing alone on a winter sea,

> þær ic ne gehyrde   butan hlimman sæ,
> iscaldne wæg.   Hwilum ylfete song
> dyde ic me to gomene,   genetes hleoþor
> ond huilpan sweg   fore hleahtor wera,
> wæw singende   fore medodrince.

> _(Seafarer,_ 18–22)

At worst the exile's situation is like damnation itself. We recall the
plight of Grendel, "forscrifen" by God in His feud with Cain and all
his progeny _(Beowulf,_ 99–110) and driven far from man. Grendel may
exercise his spite on the Danes of Hrothgar's hall, but "no he þone
gifstol gretan moste,/maþðum for Metode, ne his myne wisse" _(Beowulf,_ 168–69). With _Beowulf_ line 169b compare the _Wanderer_ line
27b. The Wanderer speaks of trying to search out

> hwær ic feor oþþe neah   findan meahte
> þone þe in meoduhealle   min mine wisse. . . .

> _(Wanderer,_ 26–27)

The dreadful sorrow of being removed from one's lord, and the joy of
being close to him, illustrated in Grendel's hopelessness and the faithful Hrothgar's hope for the future, are the trigger for the _Beowulf-_
poet's moralizing aside to his audience.

Wa bið þæm ðe sceal

þurh sliðne nið   sawle bescufan
in fyres, fæþm,   frofre ne wenan,
wihte gewendan!   Wel bið þæm þe mot
æfter deaðdæge   Drihten secean
ond to Fæder fæþmum   freoðo wilnian!

(Beowulf, 183b–188)

The same formula at the same extension of the Germanic theme of exile appear in the *Wanderer:*

Wel bið þam þe him are seceð,

frofre to fæder on heofonum,   þær us eal seo fæstnung stondeð

(Wanderer, 114b–115)

In the *Seafarer,* too, the Germanic theme of exile from the meadhall—in this case, voluntary exile—is treated metaphorically. To the Seafarer, the joy of earthly meadhalls is delusion; true meadhall joy is that which comes in the celestial banquet: (Here, too, the "Wa bið . . . Wel bið . . ." formula is echoed):

Dol biþ se þe him his dryhten ne ondrædeþ: cymeð him se
deað unþinged.
Eadig bið se þe eaþmod leofaþ;   cymeð him seo ar of heofonum. . . .

(Seafarer, 106–7)

The secular *Wife's Lament*[31] echoes the same formulas and expresses the same unhappiness in exile:

Dreogeð se min wine

micle modceare;   he gemon to oft
synlicran wic.   Wa bið þam þe sceal
of langoþe   leofes abidan.

(Wife's Lament, 50b–53)

Now let us return to the *Dream of the Rood.* The narrative opens in the middle of the night, "syðþan reordberend reste wunedon" (3). When we recall the usual emphasis on song, laughter, and talk in typical treatments of meadhall pleasure, we see that the word *reordberend* is loaded. From the Germanic point of view, the poet's initial situation—solitude and silence—is unpleasant; yet the outcome is better than one might expect: a wonderful vision. It is only in retrospect, when one reads the opening lines in the light of the poem's conclusion, that one recognizes the exile theme here. The theme's explicit entrance comes within the speech of the cross.

>   Genaman me ðær strange feondas,
> geworhton him þær to wæfersyne,   heton me heora wergas
>   hebban.
>   (30b–31)

Carried away and humiliated by enemies, set up as a spectacle, the cross suffers the typical exile's sorrows. The cross is hidden in the earth, but like the fortunate exile it is sought out by friends who give to it the kind of comfort a good king gives to his retainers:

>   Hwæðre me þær dryhtnes þegnas,
>   freondas gefrunon,
>   ond gyredon me   golde ond sealfre.
>   (75-b–77)

The adornment with gold and silver here recalls the adornment of the cross in the *Elene* and the parallel adornment there of victorious weapons (cf. the reward theme in *Beowulf*). And the cross soon gets even better payment, from the pagan Germanic point of view—fame:

>   Is nu sæl cumen
>   þæt me weorðiað   wide on side
>   menn ofer moldan,   ond eall þeos mære gesceaft,
>   gebiddaþ him to þyssum beacne.
>   (80b–83a)

Like the cross, Christ's retainers—the disciples—suffer the sorrows of exile. After Christ dies,

>   Ongunnon him þa sorhleoð galan
>   earme on þa æfentide,   þa hie woldon eft siðian
>   meðe fram þam maeran þeodne: Reste he ðaer mæte weorode.
>   (67b–69)

They share the condition of the Geats at the close of *Beowulf:* they will never see their prince again; their band is "small."

The conclusion of the poem, set up in the triumph of the cross after its suffering and humiliation, makes ironic use of the exile theme. The isolation and the loss of friends and comforts so distressing to pagan Germania becomes for the Christian poet a source of satisfaction. When Christ comes to judge mankind, it will be the crowd that suffers, while the isolated few will be victorious:

> Frineð he for þære mænige   hwær se man sie,
> se ðe for dryhtnes naman   deaðes wolde
> biteres onbyrigan,   swa he ær on ðam beame dyde.
> Ac hie þonne forhtiað,   and fea þencaþ
> hwæt hie to Criste   cweðan onginnen.
> Ne þearf ðær þonne ænig   anforht wesan
> þe him ær in breostum bereð   beacna selest,
> ac ðurh ða rode sceal   rice gesecan
> of eorðwege   æghwylc sawl,
> seo þe mid wealdene   wunian þenceð.
>
> (112–21)

(Compare the *crowd* and *lone individual* motifs in the *Christ* trilogy and *Guthlac*.) Precisely because he is a kind of exile from the worldly, the speaker is in a more fortunate position than other men, he says. It is his life's hope that he may seek the cross *"ana* oftor þonne *ealle men . . ."* (128; my italics). His friends and comforters are dead, but his emotion is not that of the Germanic exile. Instead of crying *ubi sunt,* the poet, exiled from things worldly, looks forward eagerly to the end of his life on earth, his exile from heaven, for in *that* meadhall

> þær is blis mycel,
> dream on heofonum,   þær is dryhtnes folc
> geseted to symle,   þær is singal blis,
> ond me þonne asette   þær is syþþan mot
> wunian on wuldre,   well mid þam halgum
> dreames brucan.
>
> (139b–44a)

The final lines of the poem close the Christianized theme of exile: "þa heora wealdend cwom, / ælmihtig god, þær his eðel wæs." Here, as in the *Wanderer* and *Seafarer,* what was bad from the older Germanic point of view is good for the Christian, for the worldly joys the exile has lost are a false happiness. Sorrow is exile from God.

The Germanic theme of heroic loyalty is also ironically inverted. Whereas in the heroic ethic men humbly bow to their beloved lord and die to defend him, "eorlas ymb æþeling," in the *Dream of the Rood* the cross resists the temptation to bow when Christ draws near (36, 43b) and proves its loyalty by *failing* to kill Christ's enemies: "Ealle

ic mihte / feondas gefyllan, hwæðre ic fæste stod" (37b–38). The failure
to bow is, in Germanic terms, an act of the greatest restraint. Recall
the lines in the *Wanderer* in which the speaker dreams "þæt he his
mondryhten / clyppe and cysse, ond on cneo lecge / heafod . . ." (41b–
43a). And not killing one's lord's enemies is equally an act of self-
restraint. Recall the controlling sentiment of the best of the thanes
in the *Battle of Maldon*. The Christian code, replacing the dictum:
"Avenge!" with the law, "Thou shalt not kill," inverts the Germanic
code. For the Christian, goodness lies in self-discipline and submission.

And finally, the Germanic theme of reward takes an ironic turn in
the *Dream*. In Germanic poetry, the loyal retainer is rewarded with
treasures—a point emphasized in the opening movement of *Beowulf*.
The cross is so rewarded in the *Dream*—"gegyred mid golde" (16) and
granted fame (80b–83). But the poet does not leave it at this. After
speaking of the cross as "begoten mid golde" and studded with jewels,
he says, "Syllic wæs se sigebeam, ond ic synnum fah, / forwunded mid
wommum" (13–14a). And after reporting that the cross is sometimes
covered not with gold but with blood, he adds that, as for himself,
"Eall ic wæs mid sorgum gedrefed, / forht ic wæs for þære færgran
gesyhðe" (20b–21a). The word *fah* in the phrase *ond ic synnum fah*
obviously means "stained," but in this context, immediately juxtaposed to the adornment of the cross, it seems to have a secondary,
ironic sense of "adorned" or "decorated." In any case, the parataxis
of line 13 (The cross was *x;* I was *y*) is a clear instance of syntactic
implication. The unstated relationship between the cross and the
speaker—the uncertainty of subordination—forces the mind to an
investigation of possible relationships. The phrase *forwunded mid
wommum,* "wounded with wrongdoings" (applied to the speaker),
calls up in this context the very different wounds which Christ and
the cross have suffered. Similarly, the narrator's fear ("forht ic wæs")
has its ironic analogue in the fear which the cross experiences (e.g.,
line 21). These hints at some curious parallel between the cross and
the dreamer are reinforced later by various forms of rhythmic encoding, notably verbal repetition. The narrator's comment, "Eall ic
wæs mid sorgum gedrefed" (20b), has its startling echo in the words
of the cross, "Sare ic wæs mid sorgum gedrefed" (59a); and the narrator's remark that he is "forwunded mid wommum" (14a) has its echo
in the cross's words, "mid strælum forwundod" (63b). We find numerous parallels of this kind, some of which suggest comparison of the
dreamer and the cross, some of which suggest comparison of the
dreamer and Christ. An example of the latter is the echo of *hreowcearig*

(25a), used with reference to the dreamer's lying still "lange hwile," in the syntactic rhyme *limwerigne* (63a), used with reference to Christ's lying still for a "hwile" and supported by "meðe aefter ðam miclan gewinne" (64a) and by surrounding minor echoes on such elements as "beheold" (25a, 64a). In all cases the comparison is of course unfavorable to the dreamer. Wounded in the wrong way, "mid wommum," and decorated in the wrong way, with "synnum," he might before his dream have expected an unpleasant payment for the way in which "he him ærur her / on þyssum lænum life geearnaþ" (108b–9). There are, in other words, two kinds of reward, those suggested in the poet's contrasting phrases "of worulde dreamum" (133) and "dream on heofonum" (140). As always happens in Cynewulf's allegory, the exact connections are left partly mysterious, teasing the mind. The good deeds which save men in the heroic ethic (the *arma* theme in *Beowulf*) are not the basis of Christian salvation: Christ's blood and the blood-stained cross, brought into poetic association with the poet's sins and the wounds of his wrongdoing, become the new hope of man.

6

Christ

Modern scholarship, almost without exception, dismisses the question earlier scholars labored over, "Are *Christ I, II,* and *III* (as they used to be called) one poem or several?" *Christ I* is now usually called *The Advent Lyrics; Christ II* and *Christ III* are viewed as additional and separate poems. Professor Greenfield sums up the present view as follows:

The 439 lines which comprise this series of twelve poems [*Christ I*] begin the Exeter Book collection of poetry. Often taken as only the first part of a three-part *Christ,* since they are followed in the manuscript by a poem on the Ascension which bears Cynewulf's signature (*Christ II*), and that by one on the Judgment Day (*Christ III*), there is nevertheless little reason to believe they form anything but an entity by themselves.[1]

The evidence favoring a view of *Christ I* as twelve short poems is conclusive: all twelve have separate Latin sources—advent lyrics—and have their own quite obvious unity. The first poem comes from the antiphon *O Rex gentium et desideratum earum, lapisque angularis.* . . . The second comes from the *O Clavis David* antiphon, and so on. As for *Christ II,* it is signed by Cynewulf and has the usual signs of his mastery of stylistic ornament. *Christ III,* stylistically inferior to both *I* and *II,* is obviously the work of another hand. It is heavy with hypermetric lines and aside from moments of imagistic brilliance, is little more than a collection of ornamented borrowings from Gregory, Augustine, Caesarius of Arles, and other writers on the Last Judgment theme.[2] Surely all this ought to settle the unity question, and modern critics have generally agreed that it does.[3] But it doesn't.

Two considerations. First, despite modern prejudice, unity is not always a matter of single authorship. Cathedrals have thematic unity. So do Botticelli paintings, largely executed by students. So does John Jacob Niles' version of *Mattie Groves,* and so does the Wakefield *Mactacio Abel,* though the Wakefield Master did little more than touch up his source here and there. Second, clearly disjunctive works may nevertheless be unified. For instance, a sequence of stained-glass windows, ornamental columns, or sonnets can be both individual and interrelated. All that is required is a single theme and a single set of controlling symbols.

Both of these are present in the total *Christ.* For some readers the discovery may raise a further question—one I cannot try to answer here. If it can be shown that "panel structure" is one structural type for the Anglo-Saxon Christian poem at this stage of development, what do we do with the poem or poems that immediately follow the *Christ* in the Exeter manuscript, and follow the *Christ* without break or division in the manuscript, the Cynewulfian *Guthlac A* and *B?* *Guthlac* again is divided into parts (some critics say two, some say three) and is apparently the work of more than one poet. The *Christ* trilogy focuses on, among other things, multitudes, good or bad, frequently treating bad men as individuals as well as part of a multitude; *Guthlac,* in sharp contrast, treats the good hermetic individual and talks of multitudes of bad men and demons. Is the *Guthlac* group symmetrically adjusted to the group of poems in *Christ?* Do we have, in the *Christ* trilogy and *Guthlac,* a five-panel poem? The question may appear perverse, if not absurd, I grant. I suggest it because it shows the difficulty—and also interest—of one of the most curious problems the critic encounters in his study of Anglo-Saxon poetry: the problem of possibly paired poems or paired groups—the *Wanderer* and the *Seafarer,* the *Husband's Message* and the *Wife's Lament,* the storm riddles, and so forth.

For my present purpose, it will be sufficient to show the relevance of stylistic analysis to the question of possible unity in the three-part *Christ,* and to show, by means of this analysis, the workings of a third Anglo-Saxon style of allegory.

The case of the *Advent Lyrics,* or *Christ I,* is clear. They are separate poems, each introduced by *Eala,* but there are *twelve* of them, the numerological symbol of the New Jerusalem, their allegorical subject, insofar as Christ's second coming is allegorically implicit in his first (a recurrent idea in the poems). Moreover, they are tightly bound together by rhythmic encoding. The most cursory reading shows that the temple image comes up in lyric after lyric, that gazing eyes appear several times in different lyrics, and that the idea of *locking* comes up in Lyric 2, in Lyric 8 and twice in Lyric 9. When one reads more closely, one dscovers that the whole series is built around a few central ideas which reappear again and again in various permutations.[4] One suspects that the poet worked with his Latin originals on one side of his desk, his list of motifs—product of *inventio*—on the other. Discounting the most obvious motif of all, that of God's might as a chieftain ("hea-hengla brego, soð sigores frea . . . dryhtna dryhten," etc., (403ff[5]), one can account for every line of all twelve poems in terms of seven basic ideas. Each idea is developed in every way the poet can think of, either in connection with earth or in connection with heaven, and is worked into every sentence that can be stretched to contain it. The first, the opening emblem in the poem, is the temple, which quickly comes to be associated, through traditional iconography, with the body of Christ, with cities (the temple as castle) and with multitudes (the earthly or heavenly cities). The second is the emblem of the prison, associated with the fall, darkness, sorrow, or unwisdom (mis-understanding or ignorance of that which is hidden, covered, im-prisoned). A third controlling idea is that of *advent* in any sense—the first and second coming of Christ, the coming of law or God's spirit, and likely or unlikely comings on earth (no one like Mary will ever come again)—an idea at the heart of all human hope or expectation, right or wrong. A fourth idea in the poem is "light," associated with the sun, with wisdom, and with purity (Christ and Mary). God's function as creator is a fifth controlling idea in the poem, and a sixth is one involving singing, praise, prophesy, right naming, or reputation (an effect of what people say). The seventh and last idea is treasure or—spiritual translation of the physical—bliss. The poet's technique is exegetical *translatio* of his sources for the celebration of these ideas. As his poem progresses—or as his twelve poems progress—the poet's motifs interpenetrate until finally they become a symbolic cluster in which originally disparate ideas have become inextricable. Take the temple image, for example. In Lyric 1 Christ is described as "the cornerstone which the builders rejected, the cornerstone which should be basic to the glorious temple," then the poet describes man's sinful flesh as the fallen temple. In Lyric 2, God, who holds the "key," is asked to open up life, that is, spiritual life, as though it were a building. The poet then talks of Mary, untouched by man, and in Lyric 3 he talks of the New Jerusalem, also untouched, unsullied. In Lyric 7 he speaks of Mary as God's temple, and in Lyric 8, immediately after mention of Mary, he says of heaven, "Command that the golden gates be opened, which in past days stood locked." In Lyric 9 he talks of Isaiah's belief that no man could unlock the city gate (heaven's), then talks of how, after the immaculate conception, Mary was "locked." The shifting image establishes allegorical relationship between Christ, man, Mary, and the New Jerusalem. By means of Mary (the temple), Christ is born (the temple) to save man (the fallen temple), leading him to the New Jerusalem (the temple).

This interpenetration of allegorical ideas is the rhetorical premise of the poem's structure. Because of the neatness and extreme complexity of the poet's method, it is impossible to show how the poem works except by a catalogue of motifs. (Another reader might list these motifs in some other way, e.g., separating what I call one motif into two or more. This makes no difference to the argument.)

A = the temple, cities, and multitudes, earthly or heavenly
B = prison and fall, darkness, sorrow, unwisdom
C = the first or second coming of Christ, of Law or God's spirit, the idea of
      hope, expectation of earthly things
D = light, the sun, wisdom, purity
E = God as creator
F = speaking, singing, praise, prophesy, right naming, or reputation
G = treasure, bliss

Lyric 1
2–8, A
9, E
10, E
11b–14a, C
14b–15a, E
14b–15a, E
15b–17, C, B

Lyric 2
18–19a, A (*se þe locan healdeð*)
20–21, A, E, (man *versus* God as
  builder)
22, B
23b, E

24–26a, B
26b–27, D, B
31–32, B
33–35a, F
42–44, D, B
44b, E
45, B
46b, C
47–49, F
48b, E

Lyric 3
50–54a, A
54a, F
54b–61, D, A

58b, F
59–69a, C
64–65, F
66–70, B, C
68a, G

Lyric 4
71–87, F, C
80–82, E
81b, C
85–87, B
87bff, F
89–99a, B
99b–103, C, G
102–3, A

Lyric 5
103–15, C
104–13, D
112b, E
116–18, B
119–24a, C
120b, A
124b–27a, C
127b–29, F

Lyric 6
130–33a, F
134, D
134–35, C
135b–40a, F, D
140–41, E
141–44, C, D
144b, A
145–46, D, B
146–48, B
149–50, G, C
150–53, B
154–59a, B, A, C
159b–63, G, E, F, A

Lyric 7
164–67a, B
167b–76a, B
168–72a, F
176b–81a, B
181b–95a, B, A, F, D
195b–213, D, F, C, A

Lyric 8
214–18, C, A
219–23, F, A
224–32, E, A, D
233–38, E, D, C
239–43a, D, F, E
243b–48, C, G, D, (B)
249–55, G, C, A
256–61a, B, A
261b–74, B, C, D, E

Lyric 9
275–81, D, E, A (*ealle reordberend*), F
282–94a, A, F, C (*Nan swylc ne cwom*), G, D
294b–300, C, D
301–25, F, A, C, G
326–47, A, C, D, E, F, G, B

Lyric 10
348–58a, E, A
358b–77, F, B, C

Lyric 11
378–402, D, A, F
403–15, F, A, C

Lyric 12
416–28, E, D, G
429–39, F, D, C, G

The reader's close check on even a few of the above motifs will show that *Christ I*, or the *Advent Lyrics*, must be understood as a unified work, however disjunctive. *Christ II*, we may be fairly sure, is the work of another poet—Cynewulf. The question is, does *Christ II* belong with *Christ I* or did it merely happen to land next to the *Advent Lyrics* through the whim of some scribe?

In *Christ II*, as in *Christ I*, God is a Teutonic ring-giver; the only difference is that imagery supporting the old Caedmonic metaphor is more vivid in *II* (e.g., 440–60a), and the metaphor is more skillfully elaborated here, so that it does not seem, as in *Christ I*, perfunctory. Like the author or authors of *I*, Cynewulf emphasizes the uncovering of mysteries: as Mary, Melchizedec, and others in *I* made dark things clear, the "famous man" addressed in *II* (441a), is asked to puzzle out the significance of Christ's lack of attendants at the time of his birth, Christ makes mysteries known by parables, Job reveals mysteries in his figure of the bird, and so forth. As in *Christ I*, speaking, singing, naming, and praising are repeatedly introduced in *Christ II*. Cities and multitudes, including the heavenly host, are encoded by *repetitio* in *II* as in *I*; the temple gates emphasized in *I* reappear in *II* (576b); and so forth.

One striking difference between *I* and *II* is the virtual absence of Mary from *II*. But the subject of *I* is the Lord's advent, in which Mary has a prominent role, both literal and symbolic. She need have no such prominence in a poem focusing on the Ascension. The rhetorical devices for signaling structure in the two poems reflect the same change of subject. Whereas *Eala* signals structural units in *I* (beginning each of the twelve lyrics), the rhetorical signals in *II* are more varied, though equally formal, and appropriately involve Time as perceived by medieval Christians. The first four major rhetorical units begin with *Nu, þa, þa, nu* (440, 491, 527, 558 ["Hafað nu"], and rise to a climax of repeated *nu*'s at c. 571–99. Cynewulf then shifts to *Hwæt* as his signal (586, 627) and then *þus* (686, 744), rhetorical signals which set up static cognition on what was and is; and he makes heavy use of such phrases as *sið ond ær* (e.g., 602a) *within* structural units. The poem draws toward its close with parallel rhetorical units grounded on *Forþon* (implying "Because of what has been and is, let us therefore . . ." (756, 766, 815). The last of these rhetorical units, in which the opening theme of study returns (*Sceal gumena gehwylc . . . georne biþencan*, 820b–21), comes to its climax in constructions implying futurity—*Bið* and *þær bið* (824, 840), then gives way to a *Nu* unit (850) like that with which the poet began. There are twelve formal rhetorical units in the poem.

All of these changes of focus and method, as well as the added ornaments—the rhymes, for instance—lead us to suspect that *Christ II* is a separate poem from *Christ I*. Nevertheless, *Christ II* uses the same

organizing ideas as those which unify the *Advent Lyrics,* or *Christ I.*
Here is a rough catalogue of the poem's motifs:

A = the temple, cities, and multitudes, earthly or heavenly
B = prison and fall, darkness, sorrow, unwisdom
C = the first or second coming of Christ, of Law or God's spirit, the idea of
        hope, expectation of earthly things
D = light, the sun, wisdom, purity
E = God as creator
F = speaking, singing, praise, prophesy, right naming, or reputation
G = treasure, bliss

440–c.45, D	546a, G	664–81, G
448b–49, C	547–54, D	684a, D
449b–51a, F	549b, A	686, G
460a, G	552b, A	687, E
461b, A	553a, A	691b–701a, D
462b, G	556a, G	703b–9, B
463, D	558b, B	712–14, F
468b, F	561–63, B	720–23a, C
468a–71a, F	568–70, B	731, A
471b–72a, E	569, A	731–36a, B
473b, G	572a, G	738b, A
476–80, C	574b, A	740b–42, C
478a, G	579a, E	742a, D, A
481–83, F	585, D	742b, A
482b, A	588–91, B	750a, A
492–94a, A	592, D, B	746b–51a, F
499a–502a, B	593b, B	762–65a, B
502b–4a, F, E	594, F	776b–77a, E
504b–8a, D	598–99, F	777b–78, F
512–61, C	600–603, F	779–81a, B
515b, A	602b, E	783b, B
519, A	604–11b, G	785b–89a, C
521, D	606b–8a, D	789b–96, B
523–27, C	611b–12, F	829b–33a, B, A
524b, A	621–29a, B	833a, A
530a, A	621a, E	839, E
530b, C	629b–32, A	842b, G
533b, A	650a, C	843b, A
534b, A	650b–53, F	844b–47a, G
535a, B	656b, E	847b–49, D
537b–40a, B	659b, E	858b–60a, C
540b–45, C	662–63, F	860b, G
542a, A	662b, D	861a, D

Beside Cynewulf's *Christ II, Christ III* is an inferior work, perhaps inferior even to its apparent source, the *Apparebit repentina dies magna Domini*[5]; but it develops logically out of the closing ideas in *Christ II,* and it treats the same cluster of motifs which informed *Christ I* and *II,* as the following incomplete list shows:

867–74, G, B, C, E	1007–13a, C	1199–1200, D
876a, A	1008b, A	1204–7, B
877a, D	1012b, D	1219a, D, E
877b, G	1013a, A	1226a, E
880–85, D, F	1018a, D	1228b, A
887a, A	1020, D	1229–31, B
888a, B	1021b–22a, B	1238–41, D
889b–92a, B	1030, C	1239b, A
892b–96a, C, B, D	1036b, D	1243–46, G
894b–95, A	1039–42a, E	1248a, A
896b–99, B, D	1040b, A	1248b–54, B
899–904, C, D, E	1042b–44a, B	1255, F
905–9, C	1043a, D	1257, B
908a, B	1049–56a, D	1258–61, G
910–17, D, F	1058a, D	1262–1300, B
819–20, B	1058b–59a, B	1276a, D
921–29, D, B	1069a, A	1277a, A
924b–25a, E	1072a, G	1286, F
926b, A	1076b, D	1291b, D
927b, A	1077b–79a, G	1311b, A
928b, D	1081–82, B	1334a, A
929, A	1085a, D	1334b, D
930a, E	1088a, D	1335b, D
930b–40, B	1088b, B	1339a–61, G
933, D	1089, D	1346b, D
934a, D	1090–91a, B	1362–64, B
935b, D	1091b–92, F	1365–68a, G
937a, D	1101–2, D	1368b–74, B
939a, D	1101–6, B	1375–76a, B
941b, A	1123a, B	1377–78a, A
941–44a, C	1132b, D, B	1379–81a, E
944a, A	1133b–34a, A	1381b–84a, G
946–47a, B	1136b, A	1384b–85a, B
956, A	1147–50, D	1386–87a, E
957–71, B	1160b–61a, E	1387b, G
968a, D	1161b–62a, A	1391, D
977a, A	1169–70, E	1395b, E
995–96, G	1176b–77, D	1396–98a, B
988–1006, B	1190–98, D	1398b–1402, G

1403–18a, B	1532b, A	1617a, E
1422b–26a, B	1535a, A	1635a, D
1426b, D	1550b–51a, D	1642b, D
1428–62, B	1559–77, B	1646b, D
1463, D	1569a, A	1658b, A
1465–67a, B	1579b, D	1659a, F
1467b, D	1584b, D	1651b, D
1485a, B	1587b, G	1653a, A
1489–90, B	1593–98a, B	1656b, B
1499–1509, G	1603b–33, B	1657a, D
1518, A	1607a, A	1661b, D
1519–48, B	1613a, A	1664a, A

The above catalogues of motifs suggest that the *Advent Lyrics, Christ II,* and *Christ III* are a single work, though one made up of parts which are capable of standing alone. Whether the interrelationship of the parts was planned in advance by someone who thought out the scheme as a master painter thought out his painting or an abbot thought out the plan of his cathedral, or whether the interrelationship was "revised in," so to speak, we cannot say. If the commonly accepted conjectural dates of the poems are anywhere near right (which I doubt), the latter alternative seems more likely, since the master poet's plan would hardly have taken so long to execute. But the theory that one poet (Cynewulf, say) revised two older poems to bring them into iconographic relationship with a third, his own, has a certain plausibility in the light of Anglo-Saxon poetic practice in general. In *Deor* it is clear that the poet borrowed snatches from five old stories (all possibly symbolic, as some critics have felt) and a snatch of gnomic verse, then joined these by means of a refrain and a biographical comment. In the *Wanderer* and the *Seafarer,* as we mentioned earlier, we probably have old poems rewritten or retouched to carry Christian meaning. And in all Caedmonic poetry, as in Cynewulf's *Elene,* we have the product of exegetical principles of *translatio*—the amplification, curtailing, and ornamentation of source material for some thematic purpose. It would not be surprising to find a poet, whose education and literary tradition both favored the recasting and modification of old materials for some new purpose, turning separate old poems into companion pieces. Furthermore, neat juxtaposition is highly valued in all Anglo-Saxon Christian arts. One sees this in the balance of the Elene story and Cynewulf's autobiographical conclusion, or in the dragon episode's echoes of earlier monster episodes in *Beowulf.* One sees it, too, in the visual art of the period, for instance

in the allegorical juxtaposition on the front panel of the Franks
Casket, familiar to all students of Old English since Greenfield made
it his frontispiece. On the right-hand panel stands an Adoration of
the Magi, identified by runes for *Magi*, ᛗᚫᚷᛁ ; on the left-hand panel
the artist has a scene involving Weland the Smith after he has killed
King Niohad's sons and made cups of their skulls. Weland holds one
cup with tongs (signifying its purification by fire) and offers another
to the King's daughter, Beaduhild (a gift signifying victory over her
enemies). An attendant, perhaps Weland's brother Egill, is catching
birds with which to make wings for escape (pagan Germanic parallel
to the "escape" provided by the Incarnation). The juxtaposed panels,
each representing escape from the grave (one figuratively, one more or
less literally, since Christ's coming establishes that escape), are in turn
juxtaposed to a runic inscription in alliterative verse emphasizing the
dreadfulness of death's power in the world: "The ocean cast up the
fish on the cliff-bank; the whale became sad where he swam aground
on the shingle. Whale's bone." Whatever the precise nature and meaning of these juxtapositions, it is clear that allegorical juxtaposition
was pleasing to Anglo-Saxons.

In the *Advent Lyrics,* and in the three-part *Christ* taken as a whole,
the allegorical method is neither *linear* nor *vertical* but *circular*. This
effect is achieved, like linear allegory, by rhythmic encoding, but it is
a very different effect. The relationship between the exiles of Lucifer,
Adam and Eve, Cain, and so forth in *Genesis A* is *logical,* each exile
showing the operation of the same moral principles of cause and
effect. The relationship between, say, the seafarer and the ascetic
Christian traveling through the mutable world, is *metaphoric:* each is
in revealing ways like to the other, so that the two may be discussed
as one, though they are not. But the relationship between Christ, man,
the Virgin Mary, the New Jerusalem, and earthly cities, all summed
up in the figure of the temple, is *mystical*. Specific matters of cause
and effect are no longer of interest to the poet: men are simply bad or
good, not specified as bad or good according to fully elaborated
principles (e.g., loyalty or disloyalty to chief and kinsmen). In other
words, the poet's purpose in poems like *Christ* is not exploration but
celebration: warring principles in the world of Manyness are myste-
riously resolved in one mystical sense of holiness, a mystical timeless
instant in which the Advent, Ascension, and Judgment are one event.
In this last phase of Anglo-Saxon Christian verse, the world (actuality)
is neither a model by means of which a higher code can be understood,
as in Caedmonic poetry, nor a useful metaphor, as in the *Seafarer,*

but an obstacle standing in the way of true vision; it is an impediment which must be broken down, fragmented, rearranged, smashed through. In the realm beyond things physical everything is the temple, which is the sun, which is all sound, which is all time and space in an eternal instant, which is the creator-destroyer God.

The technique is not really Cynewulf's invention, nor was Cynewulf the first Anglo-Saxon poet to use it. Christ's image of himself as a temple, elaborated by St. Paul, was frequently employed and further elaborated by medieval exegetes and artists; and one variation on the *topos* occurs in *Beowulf*. I have mentioned already the *Beowulf*-poet's double allegory of the meadhall: it is identified first with the world (God's meadhall), then with man (in which reason is the guardian, and lower faculties are potential enemies). Soon after "Hrothgar's sermon," as it has been called, in which Hrothgar first talks of man as if he were a meadhall, then talks of death, there occurs a brilliant and curious passage:

> Geat wæs glædmod,   *geong sona to,*
> setles *neosan,*   swa se snottra heht.
> þa wæs eft swa ær   ellenrofum,
> fletsittendum   fægere gereorded
> *niowan stefne.—*   Nihthelm *geswearc*
> deorc ofer dryhtgumum.   Duguð eal *aras;*
> wolde blondenfeax   beddes *neosan,*
> *gamela Scylding.*   Geat unigmetes wel,
> rofne randwigan   *restan* lyste;
> *sona* him *seleþegn*   *siðes wergum,*
> *feorrancundum*   *forð wisade,*
> se for andrysnum   ealle beweotede
> þegnes þearfe,   swylce þy dogore
> heaþoliðende   habban scoldon.
>   *Reste* hine þa rumheort;   reced hliuade
> geap ond goldfah;   gæst inne swæf,
> oþ þæt hrefn blaca   heofones wynne
> blidheort bodode.   Da com beorht *scacan*
> [*scima ofer sceadwa*];   scaþan *onetton,*
> wæron æþelingas   eft to leodum
> *fuse to farenne;*   wolde feor þanon
> cuma collenferhð   ceoles *neosan.*
>
>   (*Beowulf,* 1785–1806; my italics)

This passage marks the end of the Grendel–Grendel's dam section of the poem: Beowulf has brought peace and security to the Danes. But the passage is anything but peaceful. It bristles with words implying haste, restless motion, decline—the words italicized above—and it is alive with ironies which reverberate outward to the whole of the poem. Part of the restlessness of the passage comes from motion conflict (night lowers, the men rise); more comes from the poet's sudden reversal, here, of emotions previously associated with certain of his *kosmoi:* night is now not a threat but a protector; dawn now brings not sorrow but joy—yet is ironically ushered in by the raven, previously associated with war and sorrow. Allegorical overtones intensify the irony—what the raven (a stock death symbol) brings is *heofones wynne,* a phrase ambiguous because it might be either metaphoric or literal. As men hurry restlessly, the world too hurries—as if toward its death, one feels. The reasons for the feeling are complex, but two causes are worth remarking; the *neosan* pattern (1786, 1791, and 1806) subliminally recalls an earlier *neosan* pattern, the ominous passage which began, "Gewat ða neosian, syþðan niht becom, / hean huses, hu hit Hring-Dene / æfter beorþege gebun hæfdon" (115–17), and which closed with the words *wica neosan* (125b). Another reason the passage seems ominous is the allegorical ambiguity of the lines beginning "Reste hine þa rumheort;   reced hliuade . . ." (1799). *Rumheort* of course means "the brave or large-hearted one," Beowulf. But the hall is named Heorot, and the allegorical equation of man and meadhall was only a moment earlier established for the audience, in Hrothgar's speech of advice. So "Reste hine þa rumheort" seems to mean two things at once, "Beowulf rested" and "Heorot rested"; and because of the earlier association of the hall and the world (God's hall), the line seems to mean three things at once: "Beowulf, Heorot, and the world rested." The passage foreshadows the ambiguous language of the dragon episode, in which Beowulf's meadhall burns, then Beowulf burns, and an Armageddon allusion lies just below the surface.

This mystical rather than logical or metaphoric form of allegory appears at various points in *Beowulf.* But there is a major difference between the *Beowulf*-poet's use of this "circular" allegory and Cynewulf's use of the same thing. In *Beowulf* it is supportive, not central: it provides lyrical climaxes (some of the finest moments in the poem), it pushes the listener beyond thought to religious and aesthetic ecstasy; but because it is only one stylistic element among many in the poem, it does not suggest abnegation of thought for mystical release, escape from reality for pure celebration.

7

Epilogue

The progress of Anglo-Saxon Christian style may be viewed as a matter as much cultural as technical. Broadly speaking, Caedmonic poetry is the poetry of intellectual conversion: relationships between Teutonic and Christian thought are worked out in such a way that the Teutonic audience can easily understand and appreciate Christian ideas which might otherwise seem foreign and unnatural. The second phase of Christian poetry in Old English is, loosely, sermonic: it invites a firmly converted and devout audience to consider and reaffirm its beliefs, the poetry presenting images summing up those beliefs— such images as the storm, the whale, the phoenix, the seafarer, the exiled wife. Related to this stylistic phase but moving beyond it is the essentially philosophical *Beowulf,* a poem in which all three basic styles in allegory, linear, vertical, and circular, serve as means for exploring the nature of man and celebrating his relationship to God. The same fundamental technique, though the philosophical result is more shallow, informs Cynewulf's *Elene.* Whatever the original audience of poems like *Beowulf, Elene,* or, say, *Andreas* may have been, it is clear that the authors of these poems were less concerned with reaching all men than were Caedmonic poets: their rhythmic encoding is far more subtle than that in Caedmonic poetry; their *kosmoi* or key images, etc., are frequently very obscure indeed—e.g., the allegorical monsters in *Beowulf,* or the allegorical function of the narrator in *Elene.* These are poems of thought and exploration, poems in which drama and idea are one, with no explicit *moralitas* to guide the un-educated or unreflective reader. The last phase of Anglo-Saxon Christian verse, represented by the three-part *Christ* and, I suggest, such works as the two-part *Guthlac,* is poetry of the cell. It is poetry strictly for the greater glory of God, and if an audience was ever meant to hear it that audience was not meant to learn by it or meditate on it but only to rise through its ornaments, its holy mad-ness, to religious entrancement.

As I have tried to show, certain basic attitudes and techniques appear throughout the Anglo-Saxon Christian poetic tradition, others arise one by one within the tradition. The most obvious of the techniques used from the beginning of the tradition to the Norman Conquest is the juxtaposition of Christian and pagan experience, especially the Caedmonic juxtaposition of Teutonic kingship and God's kingship, Teutonic exile and exile from bliss. There are many others worthy of closer investigation, though I have not been able to treat them here. One is the metaphor of song; another is the "ruin" *topos;* yet another is the well-known but not yet adequately studied motif of *ubi sunt.* Among techniques which seem to have arisen during the process of the development of the literary tradition are the methods of vertical and circular allegory, supplements of the older linear method. On the particular stylistic means which make these kinds of allegory possible—rhythmic encoding, syntactic implication, the manipulation of *kosmoi,* and structural implication (the "panel structure" of the *Advent Lyrics,* etc.) I have said more than enough already.

This stylistic study, as I said at the outset, raises as many questions as it answers; it also points directions in which some of the answers may be sought. The investigation here of rhythmic encoding in two Caedmonic poems and one quasi-Caedmonic poem (*Christ and Satan*) shows the importance of verbal repetition in Caedmonic writing and suggests that similar examinations of *Exodus, Juliana,* and other such works would be profitable. The same method needs to be applied to all other long poems in Old English—especially, of course, *Beowulf.* And the apparent but as yet undemonstrated relationship between Anglo-Saxon poetic practice and exegetical rhetoric, especially with regard to the principles of *translatio* and the specific methods of *amplificatio,* suggests (not for the first time, of course) that all of this poetry needs to be examined more closely in relation to rhetorical tradition. The motif analysis here of the three-part *Christ* suggests that such analysis needs to be done on *Guthlac* and other poems which may be juxtaposed structures. And, finally, the very general similarity of stylistic evolution in Anglo-Saxon England and roughly contemporary practice on the Continent, briefly treated in Chapter 1, "Premises," indicates that a comparative approach to all the poetry of early Christian Europe might be illuminating. Such study might help to make possible a more precise understanding of the stylistic relationship of pagan and Christian poetry in the early Middle Ages. All that I leave to others. What I hope I have shown—as the proportions of my chapters may suggest—is some part of what led up to, and what descended from, the greatest poem in Old English.

Notes
Index

Notes

1 PREMISES

1. In recent years, numerous scholars have suggested that Anglo-Saxon poets may have depended heavily on classical Greek and Latin models and on classical rhetorical theory as transmitted and modified by Christian writers. See, for instance, Margaret Schlauch, "*The Dream of the Rood* as Prosopopoeia," in *Essays and Studies in Honor of Carleton Brown* (New York, 1940), pp. 23–34, rpt. in *Essential Articles for the Study of Old English Poetry*, ed. Jess B. Bessinger, Jr., and Stanley J. Kahrl (Hamden, Conn., 1968), pp. 428–41; J. E. Cross, "On the Genre of *The Wanderer*," *Neophilologus* 45 (1961), 63–75, rpt. in Bessinger and Kahrl, pp. 515–32; J. C. Pope, "Dramatic Voices in *The Wanderer* and *The Seafarer*," in *Franciplegius: Medieval and Linguistic Studies in Honor of Francis Peabody Magoun, Jr.*, ed. Jess B. Bessinger, Jr. and Robert P. Creed (New York, 1965), pp. 164–93, rpt. in Bessinger and Kahrl, pp. 533–70. Arguments that Old English poetry leans heavily on patristic exegesis and rhetorical theory are common and, on the whole, convincing. The extreme presentation of the case is B. F. Huppé's *Doctrine and Poetry: Augustine's Influence on Old English Poetry* (Albany, N.Y., 1959); but if Huppé seems at times to go a trifle too far, his general position is strongly supported by writers like Morton W. Bloomfield in, for instance, "*Beowulf* and Christian Allegory: An Interpretation of Unferth," *Traditio* 7 (1949–51), 410–15, and R. E. Kaske in, for instance, "The *Eotenas* in *Beowulf*," *Old English Poetry: Fifteen Essays*, ed. Robert P. Creed (Providence, R.I., 1967), pp. 285–310; and a number of scholars have made it seem very likely that Anglo-Saxon poets were equally familiar with writers like Boethius, for instance B. J. Timmer, in "Wyrd in Anglo-Saxon Prose and Poetry," *Neophilologus* 26 (1940), 24–33 and 27 (1941), 213–38, rpt. in Bessinger and Kahrl, pp. 124–58; and, more recently, Alain Renoir, in "The Self-Deception of Temptation: Boethian Psychology in *Genesis B*," in *Old English Poetry*, ed. Creed, pp. 47–68.

But for all the influence of classical and Christian rhetorical theory, the poems also show the influence of Germanic rhetorical theory—though no two critics seem to agree on just what is Germanic or exactly what Germanic theory was. When the principles of Parry and Lord in the thirties were later applied to poetry in Old English, those principles made it seem evident that Anglo-Saxon poetry was, without exception, oral and formulaic. Francis P. Magoun, Jr., could write with full confidence in 1953: ". . . the recurrence in a given poem of an appreciable number of formulas or formulaic phrases brands the latter as oral, just as a lack of such repetitions marks a poem as composed in a lettered tradition. Oral poetry, it may be safely said, is composed entirely of formulas, large and small, while lettered poetry is never formulaic, though lettered poets occasionally consciously repeat themselves or quote verbatim from other poets in order to produce a specific rhetorical or literary effect" (Magoun, "The Oral-Formulaic Character of Anglo-Saxon Narrative Poetry," *Speculum* 28 (1953), 446, rpt. in Bessinger and Kahrl, pp. 319–51). To get at German rhetorical theory, it seemed, one need only study the formulas in Anglo-Saxon poetry, figuring out, for instance, how a poet might, by simple manipulation of formulas and certain approved metrical structures, i.e., half-lines, create out of his head and *on the spot* such complicated verse. This was the work attempted by, among others, Stanley B. Greenfield, in "The Formulaic Expression of the Theme of 'Exile' in Anglo-Saxon Poetry," *Speculum* 30 (1955), 200–206; Robert P. Creed, in "The Making of an Anglo-Saxon Poem," *English Literary History* 26 (1959), 445–54; and Robert E. Diamond, in "Theme as Ornament in Anglo-Saxon Poetry," *PMLA* 76 (1961), 461–68 (all rpt. in Bessinger and Kahrl, pp. 352–92). The trouble was (and is), as Claes Schaar pointed out in 1956, that the two propositions "All oral poetry is formulaic" and "All formulaic poetry is oral" are not equatable. (See Schaar, "On a New Theory of Old English Poetic Diction," *Neophilologus* 40 (1956), 301–5.) As Robert D. Stevick points out, partly summarizing Schaar, the texts we have may be "the products of a transitional period, when there were written texts and lettered poets . . . using and modifying the oral-formulaic materials; there may indeed be influence, in the common literary sense, of one poet drawing on the text of another rather than drawing solely from the common formula stock (Stevick, "The Oral-Formulaic Analyses of Old English Verse," *Speculum* 37 [1962], 382–89, rpt. in Bessinger and Kahrl, pp. 393–403; cf. Jackson J. Campbell, who finds *The Seafarer* neither plainly oral nor plainly lettered, in "Oral Poetry in *The Seafarer*," *Speculum* 35 [1960], 87–96; and see also Wayne A. O'Neill, "Another Look at Oral Poetry in *The Seafarer*," *Speculum* 35 [1960], 596–600). For summary of the research, see Michael Curschman, "Oral Poetry in Medieval English, French, and German Literature: Some Notes on Recent Research," *Speculum* 42 (1967), 36–52.

The more we study Creed's desperate attempts to prove that a poem like *Beowulf* could be made up on the spot (in "The Making of an Anglo-Saxon Poem" and other essays, e.g., "The Singer Looks at his Sources," *Studies in Old English Literature in Honor of Arthur G. Brodeur,* ed. Stanley B. Greenfield [Eugene, Oregon, 1963], pp. 44–52; and "The Art of the Singer: Three Old English Tellings of the Offering of Isaac," *Old English Poetry*, pp. 69–92), or, for that matter, the more carefully we look at the supposed similarity of Homer's great epics and the tedious, long-winded oral poetry of Yugoslavia in the thirties—the comparison urged by Parry and Lord—the more doubtful we become that the better of the surviving Anglo-Saxon poems, to say nothing of the *Iliad* and *Odyssey*, were composed orally and not with a pen. I for one must throw out as unthinkable the notion that this poetry was orally composed; but there can be no doubt that, though written down from the first line forward, poems like *Beowulf* borrowed traditional oral devices. Though I very much doubt that there are two "dramatic voices" in *The Wanderer* and *The Seafarer*, I am sure J. C. Pope is right in claiming that these poems were written by poets (or, perhaps, one poet) "who understood the ancient feelings and attitudes of his people, and also the intellectual and spiritual claims of the new age" (p. 562 in Bessinger and Kahrl), and that his understanding included the two rhetorics. The availability of classical rhetoric is already well documented and its appearance in the poetry has been frequently noted, though its origin is uncertain. If we are ever lucky enough to isolate the Germanic strain, it will probably be on the basis of careful comparative studies of various currents in the Germanic stream—the kind of study represented by A. J. Bliss's "The Origin and Structure of the Old English Hypermetric Line," *Notes & Queries* 19 (1972), 242–48.

2. Marius Victorinum, in *Grammatici latini*, ed. H. Keil (Lepizig, 1870–80), 6: 188.

3. See also the definitions of Audax (Kiel, *Grammatici latini* 7: 321), Servius on Donatus (Ibid., 4: 486), Asper (Ibid., 5: 547), and Dositheus (Ibid., 7: 376).

4. See Augustine, *De doctrina christiana*, in the *Patrologia latina* and in the *Vienna Corpus Scriptorum ecclesiasticorum latinorum*. For brief comment see C. S. Baldwin, *Medieval Rhetoric and Poetic to 1400* (Gloucester, Mass., 1959), pp. 51 ff.

5. For cursory discussion see Jean Seznec, *The Survival of the Pagan Gods: The Mythological Tradition and Its Place in Renaissance Humanism and Art*, trans. B. F. Sessions (New York, 1953), pp. 84–103. For more elaborate discussion, see Rosemond Tuve, *Allegorical Imagery: Some Mediaeval Books and Their Posterity* (Princeton, N.J., 1966); Angus Fletcher, *Allegory: The Theory of a Symbolic Mode* (Ithaca, N.Y., 1964), containing an excellent bibliography; and Edwin Honig, *Dark Conceit: The Making of Allegory* (Evanston, Ill., 1959).

6. Quoted by Georg Zappert in *Virgil's Fortleben in Mittelalter* (Vienna, 1851).

7. Donatus' commentary on the *Aeneid* came as no shock in its time. Jerome, Donatus' pupil, says it was in regular use in the schools, and Servius preserves parts of it as stock information. (Cf. Domenico Comparetti, *Vergil in the Middle Ages*, trans. E. F. Benecke [London, 1895], pp. 55 ff.) On the allegorizing of Virgil, see H. C. Coffin, "Allegorical Interpretation of Virgil with Special Reference to Fulgentius," *Classical Weekly* 15 (1922), 33–34.

8. In later times this scheme came to be identified with the tripartite soul, the contemplative life being treated in the *Bucolics*, the sensual in the *Georgics*, the active in the *Aeneid*. (See Commentaries on Vergil's *Aeneid*, Codex Biblioteca San Marco, Venice, 150, xiii. (Lat.) n. 71, col. 3; and cf. Zappert, *Virgil's Fortleben*, p. 16. Since this scheme, as I show, is central to Fulgentius' reading of the *Aeneid*, I think the idea of the tripartite soul may have been central in Donatus' statement on Virgil's process of composition and may have served as the basis of his reading of the *Aeneid*. On Servius' preservation of Donatus' theory, see Comparetti, pp. 56–57.

9. See W. T. H. Jackson, *The Literature of the Middle Ages* (New York, 1960), p. 36.

10. Cf. Jackson, *Literature of Middle Ages*, p. 27. Important Josaphat studies include E. W. H. Kuhl, *Barlaam und Joasaph*, eine bibliographisch-literargeschichtliche Studie (1894), and *St. John Damascene: Barlaam and Ioasaph*, trans. G. R. Woodward and H. Mattingley (London and New York, 1914).

11. *Sigbur-Charpat con Culand*, from "Lebor na Huidre (Fol. 37, et. seq.), trans. and ed. J. O'Beirne Crowe, in the *Journal of the Royal Historical and Archaeological Association of Ireland* (Dublin, 1871) vol. I, pt. 2, pp. 371 ff.

12. For the relationships of *The Seafarer* to Old Welsh elegiac verse see I. L. Gordon, ed., *The Seafarer* (London, 1960), Introduction. As various critics have pointed out, poems like *The Wanderer* and *The Seafarer* have Mediterranean as well as Northern antecedents. See, for instance, S. B. Greenfield, *"The Wanderer: A Reconsideration of Theme and Structure,"* *Journal of English and Germanic Philology* 50 (1951), especially p. 462; R. M. Lumiansky, "The Dramatic Structure of the Old English *Wanderer,"* *Neophilologus* 34 (1950), 104–11, an argument that the poem shows the influence of Boethius' *Consolation of Philosophy;* and J. E. Cross, "On the Genre of *The Wanderer,"* in Bessinger and Kahrl, an identification of the poem with the Greek *paramythia* and the Latin *consolatio*.

13. Cf. Stanley B. Greenfield, *A Critical History of Old English Literature* (New York, 1965), p. 219.

14. W. T. H. Jackson, *Literature of Middle Ages*, p. 50.

15. The standard view is attacked by N. F. Blake, "Caedmon's Hymn," *Notes and Queries*, n.s. 9 (1962), 243–46.

16. Detailed comment on the rhetorical traditions available to the Anglo-Saxon poet lies outside my subject, but they included the Aristotelian, the Ciceronian (based on concepts first articulated by Isocrates), the "Grammatical Tradition" (going back to Horace and Aelius Donatus), and what may be called the Sophistic tradition. For brief summary of these see James J. Murphy, *Three Medieval Rhetorical Arts* (Berkeley, Los Angeles, and London, 1971), pp. vii–xxiii, and Murphy's studies, "Cicero's Rhetoric in the Middle Ages," *Quarterly Journal of Speech* 53 (1967), 334–41; "Saint Augustine and the Debate about a Christian Rhetoric," *Quarterly Journal of Speech* 46 (1960), 400–410; "Saint Augustine and Rabanus Maurus: The Genesis of Medieval Rhetoric," *Western Speech* 31 (1967), 97–110; "Aristotle's *Rhetoric* in the Middle Ages," *Quarterly Journal of Speech* 52 (1966), 109–15; and "The Scholastic Condemnation of Rhetoric in the Commentary of Giles of Rome on the *Rhetoric* of Aristotle," in *Arts liberaux et philosophie au moyen age* (Montreal and Paris, 1969), pp. 833–41. See also Friedrich Solmsen, "The Aristotelian Tradition in Ancient Rhetoric," *American Journal of Philology* 62 (1941), 35–50, 169–90; and Charles H. Haskins, "The Early *Artes dictandi* in Italy," in *Studies in Medieval Culture* (Oxford, 1929), pp. 170–92.

17. Adrien Bonjour, *The Digressions in Beowulf* (Oxford, 1950) and *Twelve Beowulf Papers, 1940–1960* (Geneva, 1962).

18. For another interpretation see Morton Bloomfield, "The Form of *Deor,"* *PMLA* 79 (1964), 534–41. On the combination of old materials as a Germanic technique, see Creed, "The Making of an Anglo-Saxon Poem."

19. Karl Müllenhoff, "Die austrasische Dietrichssage," *Zeitschrift für Duetsche Philologie* 6 (1848), 435 ff.; "Scéaf und Seine NachKommen," *Zeitschrift für Deutsche Philologie* 7 (1849), 410–19; "Der Mythus von Béowulf," *Zeitschrift für Deutsche Philologie* 7 (1849), 419–41; B. ten Brink, *Geschichte des englischen Litteratur*, vol. 1 (Berlin, 1877). For other studies of this kind see Friedrich Klaeber, *Beowulf and the Fight at Finnsburg*, 3rd ed. (Boston, 1941), pp. cxxxv–cliii.

20. A. C. Bartlett, *The Larger Rhetorical Patterns in Anglo-Saxon Poetry* (New York, 1935).

21. On the oral-formulaic character of the poetry, see note 1, above.

22. See Angus Fletcher, *Allegory: The Theory of a Symbolic Mode* (Ithaca, N.Y., 1964), pp. 70 ff.

23. Ibid., p. 111.

24. See John Gardner, "Style as Meaning in *The Book of the Duchess*," *Language and Style* 2 (1969), 143–71.

25. Fletcher, *Allegory*, p. 172.

26. James Boren, "Form and Meaning in Cynewulf's *Fates of the Apostles*," *Papers on Language and Literature* 5 (1969), 115–22. See also Constance Hieatt, "*The Fates of the Apostles*: Imagery, Structure, and Meaning," *Papers on Language and Literature* 10 (1974), 115–25.

2 CAEDMONIC POETRY

1. See G. Shepherd, "The Prophetic Caedmon," *Review of English Studies*, n.s. 5 (1954), 113–22; C. L. Wrenn, "The Poetry of Caedmon," *Proceedings of the British Academy* 32 (1947), 277–95, and Kemp Malone, "Caedmon and English Poetry," *Modern Language Notes* 76 (1961), 193–95.

2. F. P. Magoun, Jr., "Bede's Story of Caedmon: The Case History of an Anglo-Saxon Oral Singer," *Speculum* 30 (1955), 49–63.

3. N. F. Blake, "Caedmon's Hymn," *Notes and Queries*, n.s. 9 (1962), 243–46.

4. Studies suggesting this include those of B. F. Huppé, *Doctrine and Poetry* (Albany, N.Y., 1959), pp. 99–130, and M. W. Bloomfield, "Patristics and Old English Literature," *Comparative Literature* (1962), 39–41, rpt. in *Studies in Old English Literature in Honor of Arthur G. Brodeur*, ed. S. B. Greenfield (Eugene, Oregon, 1963), pp. 41–43.

5. Huppé, *Doctrine and Poetry*.

6. See Stanley B. Greenfield, *A Critical History of Old English Literature* (New York, 1965), p. 173.

7. The text cited for poems examined in this chapter (*Genesis, Daniel,* and *Christ and Satan*) is George Philip Krapp's *The Junius Manuscript*, Anglo-Saxon Poetic Records, vol. 1 (New York, 1931).

8. Huppé, *Doctrine and Poetry*.

9. Cf. Greenfield, *Critical History*, pp. 148–50. See also Michael D. Cherniss, "Heroic Ideals and the Moral Climate of *Genesis B*," *Modern Language Quarterly* 30 (1969), 479–97. Cherniss argues that heroic, not Christian, ideals dominate and that it is the heroic ideals that "give the story moral significance for [the poet's] Germanic audience" (p. 497). For one more recent attack on the so-called "historical" school, in which Huppé is the most important figure, see Philip Rollinson, "Some Kinds of Meaning in Old English Poetry," *Annuale Mediavali* 11 (1970), 5–21. But whatever the oversights of the historical school, there is abundant evidence that Caedmonic poetry is consciously exegetical. See Thomas H. Ohlgren, "Five New Drawings in the Ms Junius 11: Their Iconography and Thematic Significance," *Speculum* 47 (1972), 227–33; "The Illustrations of the Caedmonian Genesis: Literary Criticism through Art," *Medievalia et Humanistica* n.s. 3 (1972), 199–212; and "Visual Language in the Old English Caedmonian Genesis," *Visible Language* 6 (1972), 253–76. Also, Donald W. Fritz, "Caedmon: A Traditional Christian Poet," *Mediaeval Studies* 31 (1969), 334–37; and Roberta Frank, "Some Uses of Paronomasia in Old English Scriptural Verse," *Speculum* 47 (1972), 207–26. Some of

the kinds of verbal and imagistic repetition I point out have been treated by Alvin A. Lee in *The Guest-Hall of Eden: Four Essays on the Design of Old English Poetry* (New Haven, 1972), pp. 9–80.

10. Ibid., p. 149.

11. See John Gardner, *The Complete Works of the Gawain Poet* (Chicago, 1965), pp. 61–69.

12. According to Michael Benskin, *Genesis B* itself contains a further interpolation. See "An Argument for an Interpolation in the Old English *Later Genesis*," *Neuphilologische Mitteilungen* 72 (1971), 356–441.

13. Krapp, *Junius Manuscript*, p. xxxii.

14. I am of course oversimplifying the Caedmonic method. For discussion of what I call "vertical" allegory in the Caedmonic *Exodus*—especially the *Exodus*-poet's use of submerged metaphors of the Church as ship—see Frank Reuter, "The Structure of the Old English *Exodus*," *Dissertation Abstracts International* 32 (1972), 5200A.

3   FROM THE RIDDLE TO THE CHRISTIAN ELEGY

1. On the method, see for instance, B. Smalley, *The Study of the Bible in the Middle Ages* (London, 1941). Exegetical analysis in Old English is best represented by Bede's commentaries and Aelfric's writings—the *Catholic Homilies* and his translation of the Pentateuch, Joshua, and Judges. On exegesis and Old English poetry, see especially B. F. Huppé's *Doctrine and Poetry* (Albany, N.Y., 1959), and Morton Bloomfield's "Patristics and Old English Literature," *Comparative Literature* (1962), 39–41, rpt. in *Studies in Old English Literature in Honor of Arthur G. Brodeur*, ed. S. B. Greenfield (Eugene, Oregon, 1963).

2. See Paull F. Baum, *Anglo-Saxon Riddles of the Exeter Book* (Durham, N. Carolina, 1963), pp. ix–x.

3. Riddle #25 in George Philip Krapp and Elliott van Kirk Dobbie, *The Exeter Book*, Anglo-Saxon Poetic Records, vol. 3 (New York, 1936).

4. Baum, *Anglo-Saxon Riddles*, p. 4.

5. Riddle #1, Krapp-Dobbie, *Exeter Book*, p. 180.

6. See Baum, *Anglo-Saxon Riddles*, p. 3.

7. See Erika Erhardt-Siebold, "The Storm Riddles," *PMLA* 64 (1949), 884–88. With regard to Isidore and Pliny, nothing in the riddle need be traced farther back than Bede's *De Natura Rerum*, in which the relevant ideas are preserved.

8. See A. S. Cook, *The Old English Elene, Phoenix, and Physiologus* (New Haven, Conn., 1919), lvii–lxxxv and F. Cordasco, "The Old English *Physiologus*: Its Problems," *Modern Language Quarterly* 10 (1949), 351–55.

9. Krapp-Dobbie, *Exeter Book* pp. 169–70.

10. Krapp-Dobbie, *Exeter Book*, pp. 94–113. On the *Phoenix* see, especially, Alvin A. Lee, *The Guest-Hall of Eden: Four Essays on the Design of Old English Poetry* (New Haven, 1972), pp. 120–23; and J. E. Cross, "The Conception of the Old English *Phoenix*," *Old English Poetry*, ed. Robert P. Creed (Providence, R.I., 1967), pp. 129–53.

11. Stanley B. Greenfield, *A Critical History of Old English Literature* (New York, 1965), p. 183. Greenfield's discussion of the ending of the poem is excellent.

12. Both poems have been analyzed to death. Among the more interesting read-

ings are: B. F. Huppé, "*The Wanderer:* Theme and Structure," *Journal of English and Germanic Philology* 42 (1943), 516–38; R. M. Lumiansky, "The Dramatic Structure of the Old English *Wanderer*," *Neophilologus* 34 (1950), 104–12; Stanley B. Greenfield, "*The Wanderer:* A Reconsideration of Theme and Structure," *Journal of English and Germanic Philology* 50 (1951), 451–65; I. L. Gordon, "Traditional Themes in *The Wanderer* and the *Seafarer*," *Review of English Studies*, n.s. 5 (1954), 1–13; G. V. Smithers, "The Meaning of *The Seafarer* and *The Wanderer*," *Medium Ævum* 26 (1957), 137–53 and *Medium Ævum* 38 (1959), 1–22, 99–104; W. Erzgräber, "*Der Wanderer:* Eine Interpretation von Aufbau und Gehalt," *Festschrift zum 75. Geburtstag von Theodor Spira* (Heidelbert, 1961), pp. 57–85; D. Whitelock, "The Interpretation of *The Seafarer*," *Early Cultures of North West Europe* (Cambridge, 1950), pp. 261–72; S. B. Greenfield, "Attitudes and Values in *The Seafarer*," *Studies in Philology* 51 (1954), 15–20; O. S. Anderson, "*The Seafarer:* An Interpretation," *KHVL Årsberättelse* 1 (1937–38), 1–50. In some ways the outstanding article on these poems is E. G. Stanley's "Old English Poetic Diction and the Interpretation of *The Wanderer, The Seafarer,* and *The Penitent's Prayer*," *Anglia* 73 (1955), 413–66, rpt. in *Essential Articles for the Study of Old English Poetry*, ed. Jess B. Bessinger, Jr. and Stanley J. Kahrl (Hamden, Conn., 1968), pp. 458–514. See also the articles by J. E. Cross, "On the Genre of *The Wanderer*," and John C. Pope, "Dramatic Voices in *The Wanderer* and *The Seafarer*," rpt. in Bessinger and Kahrl, pp. 515–70.

13. The same example is used by Greenfield, *A Critical History*, p. 220 #10.

14. Ibid., p. 221.

15. Krapp-Dobbie, *Exeter Book*, pp. 225–27.

16. Ibid., pp. 195–96. F. A. Blackburn's translation and comment appear in *Journal of English and Germanic Philology* 3 (1900), 4–7, cited by Baum, *Anglo-Saxon Riddles*, p. 18.

17. See Krapp-Dobbie, *Exeter Book*, "Notes," p. 364.

4 BEOWULF

1. The edition of *Beowulf* used here is that of Friedrich Klaeber, *Beowulf and The Fight at Finnsburg*, 3rd ed. (Boston, 1941).

2. Internal evidence of the *Beowulf*-poet's knowledge of the *Aeneid* is not strong. G. A. Smithson, in *The Old English Christian Epic* (Berkeley, 1910), pointed out similar methods of delay in *Beowulf* and classical epics; but the methods he treats are of a general sort and might as easily be found in Irish prose and verse. T. B. Haber offers better evidence in *A Comparative Study of the Beowulf and the Aeneid* (Princeton, N.J., 1931), in his study of parallels of phraseology, motif, and sentiment in *Beowulf* and Virgil's epic. But even the most striking parallels are doubtful. One noteworthy parallel is that between the creation song of Hrothgar's scop and that of Dido's Iopas (*Beowulf*, 90–98; *Aeneid*, 1: 740–46). This instance— the one with which Haber dramatically concluded his study—has two drawbacks. First, knowledge of a few lines from the *Aeneid* might easily come from some rhetoric of the period (Virgil is very heavily quoted in the rhetorics, especially when his words sound Christian); and second, in a widely quoted passage of his *Institutes*, Lactantius attributed to an unknown Sibyl a creation song identical in all particulars. (Lactantius, *The Divine Institutes*, in the *Ante-Nicene Fathers:*

Translations of the Writings of the Fathers down to A.D. *325,* ed. Alexander Roberts and James Donaldson [Grand Rapids, Michigan, 1951], 7: 16 [bk. I, ch. VI].) Many critics since Haber have worked on the problem, but our knowledge stands where W. W. Lawrence left it in *Beowulf and Epic Tradition* (Cambridge, 1928): "It has frequently been suggested that the new learning in Britain may be seen reflected in *Beowulf* in the influnce of the *Aeneid.* This is supported not so much by parallelisms of phraseology and incident, which, though sometimes striking, are not sufficiently close to be conclusive as evidences of borrowing, as by the great popularity that the *Aeneid* enjoyed among those acquainted with Latin letters . . ." (p. 284). For demonstration of Virgil's enormous popularity among Christians in early England, see Haber, pp. 5–19; and for more general discussion of Virgil's popularity and the reasons for it, see Domenico Comparetti, *Vergil in the Middle Ages,* trans. E. F. M. Benecke (London, 1895), and Georg Zappert, *Virgils Fortleben im Mittelalter* (Vienna, 1851).

3. See Georg Zappert, *Virgil's Fortleben in Mittelalter* (Vienna, 1851), pp. 1–22, et passim.

4. *Opera,* ed. Rudolf Helm (Leipzig, 1908), pp. 81–107. Fulgentius is listed in Alcuin's catalogue of books available at York. For discussion of Anglo-Saxon learning and for Alcuin's list, see C. J. B. Gaskoin, *Alcuin: His Life and Work* (New York, 1966), p. 39 n. 2, et passim.

5. See my discussion, in Chapter 1, under "The Scop and the Rhetoricians," of Donatus on the *Bucolics,* etc.

6. Fulgentius' dramatic technique was first pointed out by J. W. Jones in "Vergil as Magister in Fulgentius," *Classical, Mediaeval, and Renaissance Studies in Honor of B. L. Ullman,* ed. C. Henderson, Jr., (Rome, 1964), 1: 273–75.

7. *Opera,* pp. 89–90.

8. Lactantius, *Institutes,* p. 9 (Bk. I, pref.)

9. *Opera,* pp. 36–40 (II, 1).

10. For analysis of this poem see John Gardner, *The Alliterative Morte Arthure, The Owl and the Nightingale, and Five Other Middle English Poems in a Modernized Version* (Carbondale, Ill., 1971), pp. 262–63.

11. Comparetti, *Vergil,* p. 109.

12. *Opera,* p. 90.

13. See, for instance, John of Salisbury, *Polycratus,* pp. vi–viii.

14. Dante's discussion of allegory, in the *Convivio* and in his letter to Can Grande della Scala, is standard. The idea that pagan poetry may adumbrate Christian revelation was accepted even by Augustine—though reluctantly (*City of God,* XVIII, 14). Cf. *Boccaccio on Poetry,* ed. Charles G. Osgood (Princeton, N.J., 1956), pp. 39, 60, et passim.

15. For discussion of the changing fashions in allegory, see the works cited in Chapter 1, note 4, especially Tuve, pp. 219–33. Origen's use of allegory and the objections raised to elements of his method have been treated by R. P. C. Hanson, in *Allegory and Event: A Study of the Sources and Significance of Origen's Interpretation of Scripture* (London, 1959).

There were many who objected to taking the pagans seriously—Gregory of Tours, for instance (*Liber de gloriam martyrum, MGH, Script, rer. Merov.,* 1: 487–88)—but the fashion continued. Cf. *Theodulfi Carmina, Patralogia Latina,* ed. J. P. Migne (Paris, 1844–64), 105: 331–32. For discussion of Beowulf's possible typic relationship with Christ, see for example F. Klaeber, "Die christliche Elemente im Beowulf," *Anglia* 35 (1911), 11–136, 249–70, 413–48, and 26 (1912), 169–99; Morton

W. Bloomfield, "Patristics and Old English Literature," *Comparative Literature* (Winter, 1962), 39–41; Marie Padgett Hamilton, "The Religious Principles in *Beowulf*," *PMLA* 61 (1946), 316 ff; Charles Donahue, "Beowulf and Christian Tradition: A Reconsideration from a Celtic Stance," *Traditio* 21 (1965), 55–116; Paul B. Taylor, "Heorot, Earth, and Asgard: Christian Poetry and Pagan Myth," *Tennessee Studies in Literature* 11 (1966), 119–30.

16. Lactantius, *Institutes*, p. 9 (Bk. I, pref.).

17. Lactantius, *Institutes*, p. 16 (Bk. I, ch. VI; cited above).

18. See *Boccaccio On Poetry*, p. 60, an argument apparently directed against opponents of Boccaccio's position.

19. Klaeber says, "Christological typology has never been a constant exemplification throughout the whole career of an individual. The lives of Adam, Moses, or David are, for example, not Christological in every detail but only in respect to certain incidents, and even within these incidents there are oftentimes divergences." *Beowulf* (p. li.)

20. Cf. Lactantius, *Institutes*, p. 14 (Bk. I, ch. V): "Homer was able to give us no information relating to the truth, for he wrote of human rather than divine things."

21. See J. R. R. Tolkien, "*Beowulf:* The Monsters and the Critics," *Proceedings of the British Academy* 22 (London, 1936), 51 n. 28. But Tolkien saw the discrepancies as unimportant, "no proof of composite authorship, nor even of incompetent authorship."

22. Note the fragments used in *Deor*. And note that the *Seafarer* and *Wanderer*, if not old poems with Christian endings tacked on (and the concensus is that they are not), must certainly be old poems reworked for a new purpose, Christian allegorizing. Again, poetry of the school of Cynewulf characteristically weaves together a variety of old and new materials for an original statement in exactly the manner Cynewulf describes in the autobiographical section of *Elene*. We have in *Beowulf*, of course, a poet's own record of how the Anglo-Saxon scop worked. When Hrothgar's scop praises Beowulf's heroism in killing Grendel, he plays Beowulf's deed against the familiar deeds of Sigemund and Heremod.

23. Lewis E. Nicholson, "The Literal Meaning and Symbolic Structure of *Beowulf*," *Classica et Mediaevalia* 25 (1964), 151–201. Nicholson quotes lines 109–14 and explains the last phrase as an allusion to the Flood ("he him ðaes lean forgeald"). This, he says, "is slightly ambiguous in its treatment of time, for on first reading, the poet seems to be saying that the Flood was something that occurred in the past in relation to the events of the poem, but a more intense study of this passage tells us that the past tense is probably the poet's own perspective. The poet is here looking to the future and telling his audience what was ultimately to happen to this evil brood." Consider the poet's many forecasts elsewhere, for instance his forecast of the fall of Hart. Nicholson finds the same leap forward in time when he comes to the giants' sword with its story of the origin of the ancient war. Again, the reading is plausible. What Hrothgar sees is *only* the origin. It is *syðþan*—later than Hrothgar's time—that the Flood will end the war. (The sword, in other words, says nothing about the end of God's war.) This reading must surely seem as unacceptable to many readers as it originally seemed to me; but it solves a problem (How could Grendel and his mother survive if God slew all their race?), and as Nicholson shows (pp. 160 ff), the theory is probable on historical grounds, having the support of medieval tradition.

24. See items in n. 15 above and also Arthur Brodeur, *The Art of Beowulf*

(Berkeley and Los Angeles, 1960), 188–219. For a bibliography of further opinion, see Klaeber's *Beowulf*, pp. clvii–clviii. Recent critics agree, for the most part, in seeing no problem in the relationship between pagan and Christian matter in the poem. A few articles that seem to me worth special mention are the following: Joseph L. Baird, "Unferth the þyle," *Medium Ævum* 39 (1970), 1–12 (a thoroughly convincing argument that Unferth is—among other things, perhaps—the traditional trouble-making priest of Woden, *discordia*); A. D. Horgan, "Religious Attitudes in *Beowulf*," in *Essays and Poems Presented to Lord David Cecil*, ed. W. W. Robson (London, 1970), pp. 9–17; R. E. Kaske, "*Beowulf* and the Book of Enoch," *Speculum* 46 (1971), 421–31; Christopher Knipp, "*Beowulf* 2210b–2323: Repetition in the Description of the Dragon's Hoard," *Neuphilologische Mitteilungen* 73 (1972), 775–85; G. C. Britton, "Unferth, Grendel, and the Christian Meaning of *Beowulf*," *Neuphilologische Mitteilungen* 72 (1971), 246–50; Terry A. Babb, "*Beowulf*: Myth and Meaning," *Arlington Quarterly* 2 (1970), 15–28; Janet Dow, "Beowulf and the 'Walkers in Darkness,'" *Connecticut Review* 4 (1971), 42–48 (an argument that Beowulf's entry into the mere comes from pre-Christian return-to-the-womb myth, but an argument that leaves open the identification of Beowulf's rise from the mere as a figure of resurrection). See also Alvin A. Lee's *The Guest-Hall of Eden: Four Essays on the Design of Old English Poetry* (New Haven and London, 1972), pp. 171–223.

25. See Joseph Bosworth and T. N. Toller, *An Anglo-Saxon Dictionary and Supplement* (Oxford, 1898–1921). If C. J. E. Ball is correct, as I think he is, the distant place is certainly the land of the Old Testament poets. His reading of *Beowulf* 99–101 makes it a Creation Song complete to the last detail, the fall of man. See "*Beowulf* 99–101," *Notes & Queries* 18 (1971), 163.

26. See Jean Seznec, *The Survival of the Pagan Gods*, trans. B. F. Sessions (New York, 1963), pp. 11–26, et passim.

27. *Beowulf*, line 942 sq. For other possible allusions, see items cited in n. 15 and n. 23, above.

28. Standard studies of Christian iconography identify the hart only with purity and aspiration, following David's psalm. (Cf. e.g., Karl Kunstle, *Ikonographie der Christlichen Kunst* [Freiburg, 1928]; L. Reau, *Iconographie de l'Art Chrétien* [Paris, 1955–56]; Gabriel Millet, *Recherches sur l'Iconographie de l'Evangile . . .* [Paris, 1960]; etc.) Art historian Harry Bober, in public lectures at Western Michigan State University and Southern Illinois University in 1966 and 1967 argued the identification I accept here.

29. Grendel's difficulty in getting away from the meadhall at first seems literal— a reference to Beowulf's grip on his arm. But he does get away from Beowulf, and yet—for reasons I point out—does not escape the meadhall.

30. Cf. Wm. A. Chaney, "Grendel and the *Gifstol*: A Legal View of Monsters," *PMLA* 77 (1962), 513–20.

31. Benjamin Thorpe, in *The Anglo-Saxon Poems of Beowulf, the Scop or Gleeman's Tale, and the Fight at Finnesburg* (Oxford, 1855), wrongly made this phrase a complete sentence. His impulse was right, though his reading of *brecða* is impossible.

32. John Leyerle, "Beowulf the Hero and the King," *Medium Ævum* 34 (1965), 89–102.

33. R. E. Kaske, "*Sapientia et Fortitudo* as the Controlling Theme of Beowulf," *Speculum* 55 (1958), 423–56.

34. Leyerle, "Beowulf," passim.

35. See Morton W. Bloomfield, "Beowulf and Christian Allegory: An Interpretation of Unfreth," *Traditio* 7 (1949–51), 410–15.

36. This is the usual and right interpretation. But cf. E. Talbot Donaldson, *Beowulf, A New Prose Translation* (New York, 1966) p. 1, n. 2.

37. Nicholson, "Meaning and Structure of *Beowulf*," gives reasons for identifying the *garsecg* (probably Neptune) with the devil. Consider Nicholson's (p. 172) "lord of sea monsters and little fishes, king of the salty depths."

38. Adrien Bonjour, *The Digressions in Beowulf* (Oxford, 1950), pp. 44–46.

39. Donaldson, *Beowulf*, p. 3.

40. But Nora K. Chadwick suggests relationship with the *haliurunnae* (*magæ mulieres*), "apparently mis-shapen, Gothic witches, stated by Jordanes to have been banished by Filimir and his army"—"The Monsters and *Beowulf*," in *The Anglo-Saxons: Studies in Some Aspects of their History and Culture, presented to Bruce Dickins* (London, 1959), p. 174.

41. See R. Rainbird Clarke, *East Anglia* (London, 1960), p. 140.

42. *Slipe* in the sense of *graven* (of images). Bosworth-Toller, *Anglo-Saxon Dictionary* (p. 885) cites line 184 only in the obvious sense. But the secondary, also adjectival sense, might well occur to the listener as an overtone in this context.

43. Cf. "þurh sidne sefan," referring to God, 172a. What Beowulf says he will do, God really does. Cf. lines 1050–62. Surely the irony is intentional.

44. On Unferth as þyle, see Adelaide Hardy, "The Christian Hero: Beowulf and Unferþ þyle," *Neophilologus* 53 (1969), 55–69.

45. On the three-part division, see Dorothy Whitelock, *The Audience of Beowulf* (Oxford, 1951), p. 20.

46. The tension in the Finn episode, between justice and passion, is strengthened if we accept the emendation of James L. Rosier in "*Icge Gold* and *Incge Lafe* in *Beowulf*," *PMLA* 81 (1966), 342–46.

47. This point has been made by Jack Durant, "The Function of Joy in Beowulf," *Tennessee Studies in Literature* 7 (1962), 64.

48. Cf. the many references in *Isaiah*, and see the treatments of the dragon image in the works cited in n. 28 above.

49. But perhaps she is not overconfident, only hopeful. So John C. McGalliard tells me. Partly this depends on the view we take of Hrothulf, who may or may not be a traitor. For strong evidence that he is not but, on the contrary, the greatest of the Danes, see Gerald Morgan, "The Treachery of Hrothulf," *English Studies* 53 (1972), 23–39.

50. According to Norman E. Eliason, in "The 'Thryth-Offa Digression' in *Beowulf*," *Franciplegius: Medieval and Linguistic Studies in Honor of Francis Peabody Magoun*, Jr. (New York, 1965), pp. 124–38, Modthryth and Hygd are one and the same: Hygd was once vicious but is now wise and gentle. (A fairly strong argument.) For more on Hygd—her name as sign of her wisdom, and Hygelac's name as a sign of his lack of wisdom, despite his power and courage, see R. E. Kaske, " 'Hygelac' and 'Hygd,' " in *Studies in Old English Literature in Honor of Arthur G. Brodeur*, ed. Stanley B. Greenfield (Eugene, Oregon, 1963), pp. 200–206.

51. It is not true that *Wyrd* and Providence are identical in *Beowulf*—any more than Fate and Providence are the same thing in Boethius' *Consolation*. See Bertha Phillpots, "Wyrd and Providence in Anglo-Saxon Thought," *Essays and Studies* 13 (1913), p. 20 et passim.

52. See Joan Bloomfield, "The Style and Structure of *Beowulf*," *Review of English Studies*, 14 (1938), 397. The hoard comes to symbolize, she says, "the joys now to pass forever from the Geats." Durant ("Joy in *Beowulf*," pp. 64 ff) sees the uselessness of the hoard as proof that Beowulf's joy is now spiritual.

53. Nicholson, "Meaning and Structure of *Beowulf*," pp. 171–72.

54. This view of the swimming match, the Grendel's Mere episode, and the dragon fight was suggested to me by Mr. Larry Stoekel.

55. Recent critics have been much concerned about whether or not *Beowulf* is really "tragic." See Margaret E. Goldsmith, "The Christian Perspective in *Beowulf*," *Studies in Old English Literature*, ed. Greenfield, pp. 71–90, and in the same collection, Stanley B. Greenfield, "*Beowulf* and Epic Tragedy," pp. 91–105; and Adrien Bonjour, "The *Beowulf* Poet and the Tragic Muse," pp. 129–35.

5 *ELENE* AND THE *DREAM OF THE ROOD*

1. The most detailed discussion of Cynewulf's use of and departure from his sources is that is Claes Schaar, *Critical Studies in the Cynewulf Group* (Lund, 1949), pp. 24–31, et passim. Schaar does not include among his "Anglo-Saxonisms" any isolated words or phrases which elaborate source material.

2. F. Holthausen, "Die Quelle von Cynewulfs *Elene*," *Zeitschrift für deutsche Philologie* 37 (1905), 1 ff., and "Zur Quelle von Cynewulfs *Elene*," *Archiv fur das Studium der neueren Sprachen* 125 (1910), 83 ff. Cf. Holthausen, *Cynewulfs Elene*, 4th ed. (Heidelbert, 1936), p. xiii.

3. Schaar, *Critical Studies*, p. 25.

4. Cf. O. Glode, "Untersuchungen uber die Quelle von Cynewulfs *Elene*," *Anglia* 9 (1886), 271 ff.

5. *Acta Sanctorum*, ed. J. Bollandus, rev. J. Carnandet et al. (Paris, 1863–75).

6. *Inventio Sanctae Crucis*, ed. A. Holder (Leipzig, 1889).

7. *Sanctuarium seu Vitae Sanctorum I–II*, ed. B. Mombritius (Paris, 1910).

8. On early rhetorical tradition, see Chapter 1.

9. M. M. Dubois, *Les Elements Latins dans la Poesie Religieuse de Cynewulf* (Paris, 1943), p. 78.

10. *Patrologiae cursus completus: Patres Latini*, ed. J. P. Migne (Paris, 1844–64).

11. G. Sarrazin, "Beowulf and Kynewulf," *Anglia* 9 (1886), 515 ff., and Schaar, *Critical Studies*, p. 239 ff.

12. Carleton F. Brown, "Irish-Latin Influence in Cynewulfian Texts," *Englische Studien* 38 (1907), 196 ff.

13. G. Grau, "Quellen und Verwandtschaften der älteren germanischen Darstellungen des Jüngsten Gerichtes," *Studien zur Englischen Philologie* 31 (1908), 25, et passim.

14. For other instances of Cynewulf's inventive use of diverse sources for the composition of a poem see Schaar, *Critical Studies*, pp. 12–96, et passim.

15. See Schaar, *Critical Studies*, pp. 41 ff.

16. Pointed out by Grau, pp. 94 ff.

17. Charles W. Kennedy, *The Earliest English Poetry* (Oxford, 1943), p. 258.

18. Cf. Holthausen's edition, *Cynewulf's Elene* note to 156.

19. For a different view of the animal imagery, cf. Schaar, *Critical Studies*, pp. 120–21.

20. Cf. Schaar's discussion, *Critical Studies,* pp. 241 ff.

21. Cf. Holthausen, *Elene,* note to 1.288.

22. Cf. Holthausen, *Elene,* note to 1.320.

23. Cf. Cynewulf's text against the source notes from 11. 419–546 in Holthausen, *Elene.*

24. This rune has never been satisfactorily explained. The two most widely adopted readings, *yrmðu,* "misery," proposed by Kemble, and *yfel,* meaning either "wretched" (adj.), or "affliction" (n.), proposed by Gollancz, are unsatisfactory because they are too distant from *yr.* Is it possible that we should read literally, taking *yr* to mean *bow* (cf. the Runic Poem)? If so, we might interpret thus: "He mourned the bow [turned against him, i.e., Death], doomed to journey forth. . . ." For discussion see Charles W. Kennedy, *The Poems of Cynewulf* (New York, 1949), pp. 8–10 and 10n.1.

25. Quotations of the *Dream of the Rood* and other poems mentioned in this chapter are from Anglo-Saxon Poetic Records, vols. 2, 3, 6. The one exception is *Beowulf,* for which I use Friedrich Klaeber's third edition (Boston, 1941).

Previous studies of the *Dream of the Rood* have emphasized the poem's doctrinal or liturgical tradition. See for example, J. A. Barrow, "An Approach to the *Dream of the Rood," Neophilologicus* 43 (1959), 123–33; Sister Anna Mercedes Courtney, S. C., "*The Dream of the Rood:* A Doctrinal Commentary," *Dissertation Abstracts* 24 (1963, Fordham); W. F. Bolton, "Tatwine's *De Cruce Christi* and *The Dream of the Rood," Archiv* 200 (1963), 344–46; Rosemary Woolf, "Doctrinal Influences on *The Dream of the Rood," Medium Ævum* 27 (1958), 137–53. Robert E. Diamond has touched on the relationship of heroic diction and the Christian subject matter in "Heroic Diction in *The Dream of the Rood," Studies in Honor of John Wilcox, by Members of the English Department, Wayne State University,* ed. Wallace A. Dayle and Woodburn O. Ross (Detroit, Mich., 1958), pp. 3–7. To Diamond it seems that heroic diction limits the Anglo-Saxon poet.

Important recent studies of the *Dream of the Rood,* include Carol Jean Wolf's "Christ as Hero in the *Dream of the Rood," Neuphilologische Mitteilungen* 71 (1970), 202–10; N. A. Lee's "The Unity of the *Dream of the Rood," Neophilologus* 56 (1972), 469–86; and Constance B. Hieatt's "Dream, Frame, and Verbal Echo in the *Dream of the Rood," Neuphilologische Mitteilungen* 72 (1971), 251–63.

26. *The Dream of the Rood,* ed. Bruce Dickins and Alan S. C. Ross (New York, 1966), pp. 1–19.

27. Ibid., pp. 17–18.

28. Ibid.

29. Ibid., p. 19.

30. Ibid., and for full discussion see H. R. Patch, "The Liturgical Influence in the *Dream of the Rood," PMLA* 34 (1919), 233–51. The influence, though clear, is limited to a few phrases.

31. The best reading to date of this much-debated poem is that offered by Tom Davis, "Another View of 'The Wife's Lament,'" *Papers on Language and Literature* 1 (1965), 291–305. See Davis for summary of earlier opinion and full bibliography on the poem. According to Davis, the wife's plight is the result of a typical Germanic feud situation which is subtly but clearly spelled out in the poem.

6 CHRIST

1. Stanley B. Greenfield, *A Critical History of Old English Literature* (New York, 1965), p. 124. Cf. Claes Schaar, *Critical Studies in the Cynewulf Group* (Lund, 1949), pp. 35 ff.

2. See A. S. Cook, ed., *The Christ of Cynewulf* (Boston, 1900), pp. 171–77, and Schaar, *Critical Studies,* p. 37.

3. The present consensus, though probably right about the multiple authorship of the poems, is not very solidly grounded. The main studies of the three-part *Christ* are reviewed by Schaar, *Critical Studies,* who shows that again and again critics have reversed one another by shifting from one standard of measurement to another, for instance from meter to vocabulary to imagery, or simply by interpreting evidence in a different way, as when G. H. Gerould reinterpreted M. Trautmann's study of vocabulary. (See Trautmann, "Der sogenannte Crist," *Anglia* 18 (1896), 382 ff. and Gerould, "Studies in the Christ," *Englische Studien* 41 (1909), pp. 1 ff.) Differences in vocabulary in the three parts of the poem (along with other less important evidence) led Trautmann to argue against single authorship; Gerould replied, "The vocabulary of an author may vary somewhat from work to work, words may be used in one that do not occur in another, an idea may be couched now in this form and now in that. . . ." And he showed that in *Christ II,* signed by the poet, 128 words not used elsewhere by Cynewulf appear. The most interesting study of the unity question, that of K. Mildenberger, "The Unity of Cynewulf's *Christ* in the Light of Iconography," *Speculum* 3 (1948), 426 ff, argues the unity of the poem but does not deal with authorship except by implication in the title.

4. This observation is more or less standard in Christ-trilogy criticism. See A. S. Cook's introduction to *The Christ of Cynewulf* and Mildenberger's discussion, *"The Unity of Christ."* Mildenberger's conclusion is, in a sense, the starting point of my own examination. He shows that although a unity binding the motifs of the different parts of Christ—the Advent, the Ascension, and the Judgment—is difficult to find in literary documents, such unity does exist in iconographic tradition, and that this tradition reached Northumbria by the end of the seventh century. He writes, "Both the poetic material and the icon seem to indicate the working of some unifying idea nowhere explicit but inherent in the recurrent combination of the motifs, a unifying idea undoubtedly apparent to contemporary Christians" (p. 432). My method has been to identify all motifs visible to me (the temple, the sun, prison, etc.) and treat as one motif all ideas repeatedly brought into association by the poet (e.g., prison, darkness, unwisdom), then to catalogue occurrences of these motifs in the poem. My hypothesis is that if all three parts of the *Christ* trilogy have the same motifs, all in roughly the same prominence, the three-part poem is a unit. Needless to say, the appearance of all of these motifs in an unrelated poem would be surprising. The reader may prove this for himself by inspection of, say, the Storm Riddles, *Wulf and Eadwacer,* the *Dream of the Rood,* the *Ruin,* or whatever he likes. (Among "unrelated poems" I do not include the two-part *Guthlac.*)

5. The edition used is George Philip Krapp and Elliot van Kirk Dobbie, *The Exeter Book,* Anglo-Saxon Poetic Records, vol 3 (New York, 1936).

Index

Aaron, 26

Aasgaard, 30

Abel: slain by Cain, 18, 25, 68; birth of, 25; mentioned, 20, 29, 60, 68

Abelard, 2

Abimelech, 23, 28–30 passim

Abraham: story of, 20; journey with Isaac, 21; God's promise to, 23, 27; among foreigners, 26; allies of, 27; joy of, 27; pleading for Lot, 28; loyal friends of, 29; in *Genesis A*, 29, 30; mentioned, 22, 24, 37

Acheron, 57

Achilles: shield of, 12

Acta Sanctorum, 86

Adam: God's love for, 23; death of, 25; exile of, 25, 31, 115; in *Genesis A*, 29; lament of, 33; mentioned, 20, 24, 32, 131n*19*

Adoration of the Magi, 115

Advent, 108, 115, 136n*4*

Advent Lyrics: motifs in, 112; allegorical methods discussed, 115; mentioned, 106, 107, 119

Advice motif, 73, 74, 78

Ægyptus sive de Providentia, 6

Ælbert: library of, 2

Aelfric: writings of, 128n*1*

Aelius Donatus. *See* Donatus

Aeneas: as typic of Christ, 58; education of, 66; mentioned, 57, 59, 81

Aeneid: allegorical reading of, 2; moralistic interpretation, 3; Christian in-terpretation, 3; tripartite soul, 56; allegory in, 56–58 passim; storm imagery, 57; tropological level of, 58; mentioned, 5, 55, 69, 82, 83, 125n*1*, 125n*8*, 129n*2*, 130n*2*

Aeolus, 83

Aeschere, 76, 77

Affirmation technique: use of, 9

Alcuin: verses of, 2; his list, 130n*4*; mentioned, 3, 4

Aldhelm, 1, 2, 5, 59

Alethia, 4

Alfred, King, 59

Allegory: different styles, x; non-Christian methods, 2; Christian methods, 2; adaptive techniques, 6; definition, 11; through rhythmic encoding, 54; devices of, 85; Anglo-Saxon style of, 107; Origen's use of, 130n*15*; mentioned, 115

Allusion: use of, 41

Ambiguity: use of, 9

Amplificatio, 8, 86, 119

Anchises, 57

Andreas, 118

Angels: disloyal to God, 20, 23, 24, 31, 32; loyal to God, 23, 24; obedience of, 24; abode of, 97; mentioned, 19, 48, 98

Anglo-Saxon Christian arts, 114

Anglo-Saxon culture, 7, 130n*4*

Anglo-Saxon gospels, 5